Breaking Squelch:

A Vietnam Introspective

By: Stephen D. Saunders

ISBN: 978-0-9637697-2-5

COPYRIGHT, 2006, MARSH LAKE PRODUCTIONS

DEDICATION

*For Elisa, Amanda, Abigail, Aulea, Emeline
and those unborn.*

ACKNOWLEDGMENTS

A gem in the treasure of my childhood memories is the playful reenactment of triumphs of U.S. history in the yard of my classmate, pal, and neighbor – Gregg Condon. Drain-tile cannon, scrap-wood muskets and a fence-post fort were the props. Life is a circle. I am so grateful for that old friend and his incisive editing, expert suggestions, and professional advice. He levered this train-wreck onto the track. Thank you "Grape!"

I also am grateful to Ric Genthe for his assistance, professional layout and cover design.

And I thank my wife, Denise. She walked the road traveled in this narrative, too. Denise covered my backside during our nearly 40 year adventure – and sometimes walked point.

BREAKING SQUELCH:
A Vietnam Introspective

PREFACE

In July 1990 I reunited with four buddies from Vietnam. They were Gerald Brown, Mike Lewellen, Chuck Maguire and Fred Duncan at Washington, D.C. We had served together in 1966-67. The occasion of our meeting was the 50th anniversary of the formation of the U.S. Paratroopers. The reunion was emotional to the point of embarrassment. By an incredible coincidence I met the photographer of a professional-quality photo of my friend, Thomas Dougher, and me in the mud. We were on "LZ Pony" moving out on patrol. Dougher was killed in action four months later.

That same summer I relocated my law office and placed the photo on display in the waiting area. Its discovery prompted a review of my army photos. I enlarged two which include Thomas Dougher and friends Richard Rogers and Bennie Holbrook, both also killed. The enlargements hang on the wall facing my desk. On the shelves behind the desk are several family photographs. Recently I noticed that the unwitting placement of these two picture groupings reflects their prominence and role in my life. I am backed by a supportive family, and seem under the scrutiny and superintending eye of friends whose death ended any chance of having their own family, and to whom I owe a duty to remember. Here is a saga of young soldiers, chronicled in the retrospective view of a middle-aged one.

1

AMERICA THE BEAUTIFUL

The Scene

I was born in 1947 and grew up in a Norman Rockwell painting. That world and its easy ways slid off the canvas years ago. When I walk my hometown streets familiar places suggest old faces and a time simple, sure and warm. That was when the local milkman delivered milk in glass bottles with cardboard lids to the front door early each morning. Old men in sweat-stained fedoras idled on park benches, resting their hands – gnarled from plowing and husking – atop hickory canes. Nearby young boys in black high-top tennis shoes with their right jeans' leg hiked up in defiance of exposed bike chains quietly listened to yarns of dirt farming, dust bowl days and depression. Doors were not locked. Back then we took for granted that every family had a home, every home a mom and a dad. Families stayed put and stayed together. Dads had a job and most moms worked at home. Moms were not soldiers. On Memorial Day Boy Scouts camped at the Greenwood Cemetery at the edge of town and, as a gesture of honor and respect to the dead veterans, patrolled the graves at night. The older boys stoked the tenderfoots' imagination with tales of ghosts rising from the graves. During the day uniformed scouts proudly guarded the entrance road, greeting visitors with three-fingered Boy Scout salutes.

Universal values were absorbed at play, observed in adults and taught at school. We learned that an American flag must never touch the ground. It was not used for decoration or advertising. Grade schoolers pledged allegiance to it each morning before classwork as the framed faces of Washington and Lincoln looked on approvingly. The national anthem was a benediction. School taught history and citizenship and that America was the world's good guy and always had been. To be born was to be equal. To be born was to be free. If you engaged the birthright you could be happy.

During lazy summer weeks I raptured in boyish freedom at my paternal grandparents' tenant farm. The haymow pirate ship and the chicken house Ft. Apache were delights for imagination. I slurped mouth-to-water in the pasture from a tiny spring pool like the cowboys did. My grandparents' simple farm lifestyle remained little changed since the Great Depression. Grandma cooked on the woodstove. Saturday night meant a trip to town in the '37 Chevy. They traded dressed poultry and eggs at Reeder's store for the few foodstuffs they could not tease from the earth with calluses and sweat. Afterwards Grandma chatted in Swiss with other immigrants around the courthouse square. She had crossed the cold Atlantic in steerage as a child in 1898. Interlocking ties of family and friendship spun out from their life like a giant spider web attracting folks in their loving generosity. They knew tragedy; they lived hardship. They were the richest people I have ever known.

Our family went to church on Sunday, even though it was a chore. We felt guilty and were damned if we did not go. Women could not attend bare-headed; forgetful ones even pinned kleenex to their hair to get by. We altar boys memorized undecipherable and repetitious Latin incantations. For me mass was a meaningless clock watching bore. I served early morning mass on alternate week days and each Sunday. I hated it. Still, the personal discipline involved had an effect. And the altar boys filled the priest's wine cruet; I enjoyed a swig on the sly. We seldom asked why about anything serious because there was little question. Boys were troublesome, but not impertinent. Before modern disposable culture; things, relationships, and values seemed permanent. Most of my kindergarten class graduated from high school together. The doctor who delivered me visited me at home when I was really sick. I could count on tomorrow being much like yesterday. People returned refillable pop bottles to the mom-and-pop grocery store and *Gunsmoke* aired every Saturday night – year after year.

Most households had one black and white TV. All generations watched the same programs and shared similar culture. Westerns dominated TV and the Saturday B-movies and serials at the Sun Theatre in Brodhead, Wisconsin. Each episode held a moral. The good guys – with courage, effort, and sacrifice – eventually always won. The screen was black-and-white and so were the moral choices. Now it would be called gray.

Role Models

The good warrior, one who faces danger and hardship in defense of right, always trumped sports idols in my eyes. And even the public image of sports "heroes" back then did not portray players smoking or drinking, nor did they brutalize women or mock authority and good manners. World War II vets, cowboys and other stars of TV and movies showed us how a man should conduct himself in the world. Davy Crockett scorned surrender at the Alamo and went down swinging. Roy Rogers, The Lone Ranger and Hopalong Cassidy were honest, kind to horses, polite to womenfolk and never ran from a fight. American fighting men bore any hardship, braved any danger and sustained severe loss to avenge Pearl Harbor and liberate Europe. We saw it in movies such as *The Sands of Iwo Jima, Bataan,* and *The Longest Day.* Sgt. Stryker played by John Wayne in *The Sands of Iwo Jima* was the tough Marine role model. He was unambiguous, intolerant of any mid-ground between right and wrong. Screen actors Audie Murphy, Lee Marvin and Jimmy Stewart were genuine war heroes. Such icons imparted American mid-century notions of moral certainty and national purpose, and their bravery guaranteed the ultimate triumph of right.

I poured into the mold. Somehow we were imprinted with a personal honor code. The greatest generation sired us. World War II was fought and won by our young fathers. It was the "good" war waged with moral clarity. Their tales of war and service were wonderful. I was moved by them and still am. That legacy was supplemented and promoted in movies and television. The outcome was always positive, even if it involved sacrifice. Boys assimilated principles from vicarious exposure to those experiences. We knew what each other's dads did in World War II and where they served. Their souvenirs were often our playthings. We mowed down Krauts and Japs by the horde in backyards all over Brodhead. I cannot recall a time when the geography of World War II and its major campaigns were unfamiliar to me. I studied my dad's army photos with reverence and have safeguarded them since I was a kid.

The happiest moment of my childhood happened in my tenth year on a Sunday evening next door to our house at Grandpa Bouton's. He sent me to fetch a wooden box from the closet in an unused upstairs bedroom. It had been sent to him by my father from the Marianas island of Saipan in 1944, a key island battle of the Pacific war. I brought it downstairs and set it next to grandpa's ever-present ashtray at the dining room table. We opened the box and there lay a Japanese army bayonet with steel scabbard and its well-used leather belt holster. An intriguing odor of mildew and old oil, and its fierce battle-worn look, incited wonder and amazement. The weapon beheld the mystery and awe of the Second World War that so fired my young imagination. If my cronies could only see this! – I thought. I coveted that thing, but I was just a kid and it was grandpa's. Besides, it was razor sharp. I pictured a villainous Japanese soldier honing it for battle. Our 1957 meat-and-mashed-potatoes propriety was not so safety-obsessed, sensitive and sanitized as now; and generous Grandpa read my heart. He said, "take it home with you." This was better than Christmas morning. It gave a tangible connection with history. I cut myself a few times and learned to be careful. I imagined the bayonet's journey with Japanese imperialism through the far east. Did its owner serve in China before Saipan? What was his fate? How did he die? The bayonet represents a spiritual link to my father and grandfather.

The Korean War (1950-1953) is in the periphery of my memory. My friend's dad, a captain in the army reserves, was called up. My step-cousin, Miles "Mike" Zimmerman, remains missing in action there. My grandparents had a TV, but we did not. Grandma would call me to come to watch news programs about the war and try to see Mike. He had been a high school football player and a hero to this kindergartner. His death put a face on that war. We thought America was in the right in Korea, too.

Beckoned

I had little doubt that a great future armed conflict, the World War for my generation, would be waged against the Soviet block. The "Red" Chinese and Russians had replaced the Japanese and Nazis as world villains. *Exit strategy* had yet to usurp *commitment* as the polestar of foreign policy and marriage. It seemed inevitable we would all have to do our duty when and however it came. Just like Davy Crockett had done. Just like we watched John Wayne do. Then JFK told me to ask not what our country could do for me, but what I could do for it. He asked me to bear any burden and pay any price in the cause of freedom and liberty. They shot him, but I remembered his message. Those notions meshed with all that this middle class small-town midwestern boy of the 1950's and 1960's had absorbed into his bones.

2

WAR AND MEMORY

Haze

I never imagined Vietnam would stick with me like it has and affect so many aspects of my life and habits. It is always on my mind and sometimes it seems as if inside I am still there. It has been my ambition for some years to record my thoughts and feelings on the subject for my family, and perhaps for myself, too. My hope was always to resolve the experience. All my life I thought and assumed that it would somehow naturally resolve. At middle age I realize that it will not. So I now relate with clumsy wordsmithing as my mind's eye sees it.

Nearly 40 years ago I left Vietnam and have not forgotten any of it. But my factual memory is not linear; and details frequently obscure. It was bewildering. As a lowly grunt infantryman I had little idea of the big picture – where our platoon was located or its mission. So it was just follow the leader, endure the moment and get one day "shorter." Days of parched exhaustion from humping the bush blurred one into the next. Weeks of monsoon-sodden misery blended into dull and unremarkable sameness.

My emotional memories of the war remain raw. To chronicle war is not so much to try to reveal its brutal face as it is to try to understand it as a personal journey and a human marvel. Once involved in war you submit to its power, become immersed in its culture, and are bewitched by its awesome might. It does not end with the shooting. Each man fought a different war. What he beheld was affected by his knowledge, angle of vision, attitude, perspective, job, and rank. I roamed through the Vietnam War with excitement, awe, and dark apprehension – but without understanding. At age 19 I was too young to process it. Even now, looking back down the worn corridor of nearly four decades, the event does not unscramble. There remains vague and surreal images at the portal, and a pit of forceful but inexpressible emotions.

Time

Powerful explosive episodes highlight certain moments and absorb the surrounding time, smothering the memory of other experiences and events which would otherwise be noteworthy and unforgotten in normal circumstance. A 30-second firefight lasts one month. The vividness of an eventful ambush patrol fogs scores of routine ones. I confuse sequence and transpose detail. I recall when Doc Hartnell shot the NVA (North Vietnamese Army – singular and plural) with his .45 pistol, and recollect that night patrol in Tuy Hoa seeing Doc flung through the air in my snapshot vision, lit by the bright flash of the exploding booby trap that shredded his brand new fatigues. I close my eyes and see it in distinct black and white. He immediately yelled for me to see if I was also hit. But I do not recall him in any of the many other patrols we shared. Most days, patrols and "humps" are forgotten or vague from their uneventful sameness and drudgery, all run together like goulash. Yet their collective emotional impact always lays dormant within.

Vietnam time was measured in clumsy increments. Weeks passed where I was ignorant of the date or the day of the week. It did not matter. Sundays were not a day of rest. There were no days off. Crossing off a block of time on my tiny short timer's calendar, a bellwether of personal progress, was a satisfying moment. A tantalizing date – suspended up and out in time light years away – absorbed my dreams and fantasies. If body and soul stayed together for exactly one year, I would go home on June 2, 1967. That was the magic "DEROS" date (Date Eligible Rotation Overseas), a focus of comment and calculation: "In 58 days and the wake up, I'll be in single digits," or "I'm buying a new canary-yellow GTO and keeping a cooler of Pabst in the back seat." There were epochs – landmarks in time like "When Eddins was RTO," or "Just after we swept through that coastal village, deserted except for those deformed people," or "that time when we were strafed by gunships." References to dates in the past had little meaning. Time lasts longer for the young, and in Vietnam it lingers forever. So much happened, but time stood still.

Distance

The harsh reality of all facets of the Vietnam ground war was wholly alien to my previous life. You take only your character, training and strength. I adapted very well, quicker and better than I expected. That existence is so all-consuming and seemingly eternal, it removes and estranges you from home and your former life. It seems that the war is all you have ever done and all you can ever do. Family and home become a distant memory; their remoteness increases out of proportion to actual passage of time. Eventually you cannot even conjure, for instance, the sound of your mother's voice. At night I often had pleasant dreams of home, and then woke up to the nightmare of reality. The mirage cleared to an immediate realization that I may see home again only in my dreams. *There* was there and then; and *there* is here and now, and it has been in everything – everything since Vietnam! The polar opposition of that war to all other life experience induced a reflection on the obverse. When there, I obsessed on here; and now here, I imagine there. Knowing how some suffered there, and because they were there, perhaps is why I sense self-resentment when I am comfortable and at ease. It is hard to appreciate something for which there is no contrasting comparison. Vietnam gave a contrast.

You do not forget, and you really do not want to, and I resent those who pretend they have.

Withdrawal

For many years I somehow could not grasp in my subconscious mind that I really experienced the Vietnam War. Memory voodoo had cast a spell. No one would speak of it or inquire about it, including me. In civilian life as a college student there was little contact with any who had served. Student veterans then were few and invisible. Except for the nightly news, even the war seemed obscure and unacknowledged. No sacrifices by the home front were evident. *Gomer Pyle USMC*, a comedy set on a U.S. Marine base with no reference to the war, was a leading TV show. On campus in Madison, Wisconsin combat service was a subject to be avoided; and you expected to be scorned and ridiculed if it was known. And you were. Campus unrest and student violence – anti-draft inspired, but often in the guise of anti-war sentiment – in the heart of privilege and learning perplexed me. The negative community and national attitude toward the veterans spawned a personal reticence about it that endures.

I went to ground, took cover, and stayed low. But attempting to escape it is like chasing your shadow. There is no gain no matter the effort. In my 19th year I received my *real* education while fighting in an infantry platoon in South Vietnam. And, having survived one year in the field there physically unscathed, felt emotionally shucked out and incomplete by the combination of the experience and its aftermath. Like most men who fought there, I later navigated the war's hidden shoals. There were swells. The seas were sometimes angry. There were no charts. Don't trust the tide to sweep you through. Pull hard on the oars. Stay balanced. Hope someone in port calls for you through the fog. Some wreck.

Some anchor outside the shallows – the voyage itself an excuse for their personal shortcomings and failures. A few intentionally ran aground. They crowded the limelight. These phonies spit upon pride and honor.

It would be a personal waste to forever feel so intensely – just to leave it to dust like the rest of me. So now it is time to stop and face that shadow. Time to jot out some of my recollections and how I feel about them. Time to relate, after a fashion, my highest non-family honor: to have fought beside men and boys of the same resolve and willingness to sacrifice for their country as their fathers. I remain awed by what they did and forever shamed by America's betrayal and rejection of them. To give voice to their experience places a flower on the graves of my friends who died in Vietnam and in its wake.

Expression

Years ago I dreaded the time when my children might ask me about Vietnam. Perhaps they would know Vietnam as a country and not as a war. I sincerely thought that my daughters somehow would know little about it and they would never call me on it. Of course, they found out. When Elisa, my oldest child, was in sixth grade several other veteran dads and I were invited to talk to her class about the war. The thought of doing so really upset me. Usually *events* in war are what is related and that is primarily what follows. My interest and preferred focus, though, is the *effects* of experiencing such events. Those who write memoirs with talent, relating the effect of an ordeal upon them, have my admiration and envy.

In 1968 I separated from the army, but it never left me. Involuntary thoughts of action in Vietnam deviously intervene to dilute full enjoyment of life's most satisfying moments. Four decades have only softened my hard feelings. After so much time one should be able to gaze in life's rear-view mirror with dispassionate reflection and some understanding. But I have reached only accommodation and coping. My emotions, scabbed over, have festered for years and still ooze with latent anger. The war experience is seasoned by some perspective, if not wisdom. In half of my waking hours, it seems, my mind wanders. Then it hits on some aspect of Vietnam, like an auto radio scan – searching and then seizing the strongest signal. Age should bring meaning to my experience and repose from its sharper points. It brings neither; quite the contrary. Passage of time seems to aggravate anomie and anxiety. The *effects* of the ordeal are not the real problem. Rather, the issue is an inability to even approach an adequate and appropriate *expression* of the experience and its meaning. My hope is that organizing the central and formative experience of my life – and expressing an inner life centered around it – may be calming, if nothing else. This narrative is neither unusual nor of special interest. The story is universal. All is not told here. Most is not tellable. Some I decline to tell. The lighter side of dire times are the ones often highlighted in such sagas. But that just picks the white meat from the bird. I do not do that here. The carcass is not so tasty.

3

JOINING UP

"You mother fuckers have twenty seconds to un-ass this bus," screamed drill instructor SSgt. Saltzman. I'd just been welcomed to Ft. Knox, Kentucky and embraced into basic training. It was June, 1965. The most poignant three years of my life had just begun!

In our senior year Pete, my best friend, Tim, and I often hung out at the army recruiter's office in Janesville, Wisconsin – a neighboring town where we went in search of teenage trouble and excitement. As seniors without purpose we relished the entertaining bull sessions with the recruiter, Sgt. Teal, a colorful old lifer with three up and two down. My future pointed toward the U.S. Army anyway. You cannot see the world's broad horizons from home. Dependency also tunnels vision. My parents never meddled. An urge for independence and self-sufficiency made the choice easy. I did not develop other prospects and felt that a hitch in the army would earn my place in this country, not such a corny concept then. Besides, I had a wild hair that did not belong on campus and was keen to join the paratroopers. I recall a 1950's movie starring Robert Wagner as a paratrooper. While he was hospitalized for wounds a nurse remarked that paratroopers were brave. That sticks with a kid.

In the spring we three were on a paid-for bus trip and overnight at the dumpy downtown Milwaukee Antlers Hotel for a GI physical exam. Somehow we got booze and I only remember Tim tossing water balloons on the street from an upper floor hotel window. Shortly after high school graduation, we left for basic training at different posts. Pete and I spent that Christmas together

Author at Ft. Benning jump school, December 1965.

at Ft. Benning, Georgia during airborne jump school. We were only a week apart in the three-week training cycle. A year later we met in Nha Trang, South Vietnam shortly before Christmas. Pete belonged to a Special Forces "C" Team and I looked him up when I passed through Nha Trang enroute to R & R in Bangkok, Thailand. When I returned from Bangkok a few days later I spent an AWOL day with him. I treasure a photo of us snapped there crouching in front of Chinese Nung mercenaries in jump training. Tim worked in a hospital lab in Saigon. He died in the late 1970's when his motorcycle hit a bridge abutment near Albany, Wisconsin. We had fun times together and I often walk by his old home in Brodhead and remember.

Friends and neighbors since age 8, author and Pete Bernstein meet in Nha Trang in December 1966. U.S. Special Forces training Chinese Nung "Mike Force" mercenaries in parachute landing.

4

OVER THERE

Arrival

    I traveled to Vietnam on June 1, 1966 by a commercial airliner, via Ft. Dix, New Jersey; Anchorage, Alaska; and Japan. At Tan Son Nhut Airport in Saigon the choking moist heat engulfed me; the starch in my khakis dissolved in sweat. The bathrooms at the terminal denoted the state of the nation: a vile odor emanated from the fecal plugged toilets. Their novel design resembled a kitchen sink set level in the concrete floor. The user squatted over one and did his business next to several others lined up one beside the other. The flush mechanism did not work.

    The army labeled a soldier's one-year assignment to Vietnam a "tour of duty." The term butchers language. "Tour" suggests an outing – relaxed travel in a pleasant locale. "Purgatory of duty" or "gauntlet of duty" would have been more precise.

    Our planeload rode from the airport in army buses, windows screened with heavy chicken wire to deflect hand grenades. The hustle and bustle of the smoggy Asian street scene with open-air markets and street vendors was an exciting novelty. The many civilian men of military age I saw in the markets and astride Hondas surprised me. Were we here in their place?

    Camp Alpha, a large replacement depot, was our destination. It resembled a large POW camp: hundreds of men with no purpose milled about in a confined space. It was a holding area to in-process and await transportation to our assigned army divisions. McCrone, my buddy from the 101st at Ft. Campbell, and I amused ourselves and relieved boredom with a prank. We stood at any closed door of a building until a few GIs asked what lay within. We told them that Red Cross girls, "doughnut dollies," would soon hand out cold Coke and cookies. Long lines formed behind us and we disappeared to create another line elsewhere.

I soon departed for the First Cavalry Division on a C-130 transport plane to Camp Radcliff near An Khe in the central highlands. Three buddies from airborne infantry training, parachute jump school, and the 101st Airborne Division and I were assigned to Company C, 2nd Battalion, 8th Cavalry (Airborne) of the First Cavalry Division. Our infantry brigade was all paratroopers. We drew jump pay all year, $55 a month, but never jumped there.

C Company

Except for the first sergeant, company clerk, supply sergeant and a few others, C Company – about 80 men – was in the bush when we arrived. The rear-area company quarters consisted of several 30' x 20' canvas tents facing both sides of a mud street, each tent outlined by deep rain gullies. These tents were airless and steamy with that familiar canvas-petroleum odor familiar to old Boy Scouts. The climate was sweltering; it would take time to acclimate. On the hill above our tents stood the gloomy wood and screen tin-roofed mess hall, smelling sour and greasy like the home-made army bread concocted there. Among the offerings: warm re-constituted milk, green powdered eggs, and a putrid gray substance the cooks called bread. It was grub that would physic a fox. Privies were nearby as were "piss tubes" – metal rocket cylinders sunk into the ground for urinals, the ground around them spongy and seeping.

The first sergeant placed us on latrine duty, which I describe later, filling showers and other work details. Each shower consisted of an open-top 55-gallon drum and spigot framed six feet above a wooden pallet. We transferred water from huge rubber bladders at the mess hall into jerry cans and hauled them to the showers and up the ladder to the drum. It was heavy hard work for one unaccustomed to the heat and humidity.

The supply sergeant issued our rifles and equipment: helmet, butt pack, ammo pouches, canteens, pistol belt, suspenders and the like from the supply tent. None of it was new. Some lay piled on the ground caked or stained with the blood of its former owners. He sent us to the creek behind the tent to scrub the gore from the gear, and pointed out several helmets lining a shelf – each with a bullet hole.

3rd Platoon

A few days later the grunts came in from field duty – Operation Crazy Horse. They looked frightening and smelled ripe. It was the facade of a hard reality. Their uniforms were a mockery of the starchy, spit shined strict standard of stateside paratroop units to which I was accustomed. Fatigues were grimy ragged mosaics of faded dun green with overlaying gray swirls of salt stains. Their collars were caked black with accumulated neck grease that no river crossing could dissolve. Combat gear had settled on their bodies like patina. The particular appearance of each man's equipment and how he toted it and his ordnance were as unique as fingerprints. Boots were cracked and scuffed bare of polish or any vestige of black stain. Cloth helmet camo covers frayed at the rim had rinsed to tan-grey by rain, mud and sun, and were graffitied with names of girlfriends or hometowns – the 60's equivalent of WWII bomber nose art. Elastic helmet rim bands stored mosquito repellent, P-38 can openers and used grenade pins. These campaigners were gaunt and their skin blemished with sores, insect and leech bites and scrapes. Safety razor field haircuts were gouged and blotchy. I would soon resemble them. The main difference for now was internal.

Third platoon, about 30 men, was my group. It bore an indefinable collective pride and spirit. A platoon in Vietnam was an infantryman's identity, his clan. I met many new buddies that day. They were very glad to get replacements. I was warmly welcomed because more hands made lighter work. A rifle platoon is required to carry a certain amount of weaponry and perform missions regardless of its numerical strength. Nothing was ever fair or logical in the army. I sensed no exclusion or aloofness by a brotherhood towards an uninitiated neophyte. My mother had given me a small black and white striped collapsible hand mirror. It was a hit with these veterans; no one else had a pocket mirror. Life was that basic and sparse. I still have it.

These old hands seemed as eager to teach as I was to learn. They showed me how to carry gear and food. One advised me what not to take to the field. These veterans looked older and careworn. An aura of knowledge hung about them. It was lore of small, but important, things – tricks that mattered only here. They said to place cord around and under one of the five M-16 magazines squeezed in your ammo pouch. Then you could jerk it out fast without fumbling. They warned to secure your grenade pins with tape. Don't sling belts of machine gun ammo – Pancho Villa style – across the body. That made it impossible to keep the ammo clean. And how camouflaged is a torso draped in shiny brass? Carry it instead in 100-round canisters or cardboard boxes on bandoliers. Later in the bush these young old timers showed the knack to set trip flares. They pointed a way to booby trap a claymore mine with a hand grenade. They divulged recipes to make C rations palatable. The best advice: *always* have a round in your chamber.

The Leader

My platoon had no officer platoon leader. Instead we had Sergeant First Class Alonzo who had led it since the unit arrived in

August of 1965. He was a legend. That night he told us that in the Korean War and Vietnam he had earned every decoration for valor except the Medal of Honor and he would do anything to have it. The statement was presumptuous. At that time I interpreted it to mean he would sacrifice his platoon if need be. I think he would have. He was a heartless strict taskmaster and we feared him. It was said that he once swam after a fleeing VC (Viet Cong) with a knife in his teeth and dispatched him in the water. I tried to avoid his notice. I had attended RTO (radio) school at Ft. Campbell, Kentucky so had a leg up on radio procedure in Vietnam. The first time I carried the radio there was during a patrol in difficult steep terrain. Afterwards Alonzo commented with a sinister bandito sneer, "You humped that radio good, boy." Even praise made me uneasy about him.

His blood was up on a day when we spied an enemy who took flight down a trail. At Alonzo's command our platoon gave chase. Just as we lost sight of the VC he would appear again up the trail. My buddy, Mike Lewellen, who was Alonzo's mortar platoon radioman (called an RTO), filled me in on these details. I was struggling along laden with machine gun ammo. Alonzo's aggressiveness overrode good judgment and the pursuit continued. The platoon became exhausted and strung out along the route. Then an old sergeant prevailed upon Alonzo to wait. The terrain ahead, the obvious decoy, and the furtive situation was a certain set up for an ambush. Mortar fire was summoned and struck that area. The resulting enemy bodies there showed where they had lain in wait for us.

Machine Gun

I was assigned to Richard Winegard's M-60 machine gun team. Richard Rogers was the assistant gunner. The first task was to thoroughly clean the gun. We dismantled it on a poncho and

My first day with 3rd platoon at Camp Radcliff involved a thorough cleaning of our M-60 machine gun. L to R: Author, Rogers, Winegard.

cleaned and oiled every nook and cranny. I would repeat this procedure a hundred times in the coming months, a daily ritual regardless of weather or circumstance. We treated the gun like a young mother cares for her new baby. It was cleaned and carefully oiled before we ate or dug in for the night; we were its servant. It came in-country from the States when the First Cavalry Division deployed. It was the oldest of the six machine guns in the company. Much of the bluing was worn off, the black receiver cover was chipped nearly bare, the leaf spring was replaced with C-ration wire, but we kept the critical gas cylinder polished like silver and the gun always fired. Rogers soon became gunner.

It weighed 23 pounds when not loaded with a short starter ammo belt and was awkward to carry. When I was a gunner I usually carried it on my right shoulder, grasping it by an extended leg of its retractable bipod. The load caused a hard callus lump above the collarbone. I fired it left handed, sometimes from the shoulder. The spent casings ejected on the right side of the gun, so the hot expended brass burned hickeys on my neck and chest. Machine gunner was the only job I ever felt like I truly mastered in my life, and the one of which I am proudest.

5

SKYTROOPERS

The First Cavalry Division had introduced the "air mobility" concept of warfare in Vietnam. Its equipment included 400 helicopters of several types for reconnaissance, supply, troop transport, and support. Helicopters made it possible to rapidly insert combat power over difficult terrain and beyond enemy defenses, a modification of traditional infantry linear tactics. The division could recon and strike over a wide area with the flexibility to mass or apply combat power where desired or needed, without the disadvantages of dispersal and vulnerability of parachute and glider units. Once enemy contact was made, troops could be rapidly concentrated at the point of conflict. Gunships circled overhead offering direct close fire support with machine guns and 2.75" aerial rockets housed in a 48-tube rocket pod on each side. Chinook helicopters airlifted howitzers within supporting range of the infantry.

Air assaults were thus a common part of our field routine, although we walked plenty. On some days we made several air assaults. Some involved a dozen or more helicopters. When only a few helicopters were available or landing zones (LZs) were very small, these choppers shuttled us into the objective.

The workhorse of the division was the "Huey" helicopter. The transport version was called a "slick." It could carry 6-8 infantrymen with combat gear in addition to a pilot, co-pilot and two door gunners each manning an M-60 machine gun nestled in an alcove on either side of the engine compartment. The Huey had open sides to the troop/cargo area. Troops sat on a web seat in the middle or on the floor on the sides of the slick facing out and dangling their legs in the wind. Infantrymen were not belted in. When the Huey banked, those on the inside of the turn faced to earth and

A view from a "Huey" during a July 1966 air assault in Tuy Hoa.

sloped toward the ground, held in only by centrifugal force – a unique thrill! The ride was noisy and exciting. The scenic views were breathtaking, especially near the coast, but at the time I had little appreciation for such things.

While the infantrymen were en route, artillery fire peppered the intended LZ and sometimes dummy LZs nearby. When the assault slicks closed in, escorting helicopter gunships blazed away with suppressive rocket and machine gun fire. Then as the slicks were setting into the LZ their door gunners opened up, adding their machine gun fire to the cacophony. The racket and firepower was deafening. It alarmed new replacements who assumed the worst was waiting for them. They did not know that this fire preparation was routine and precautionary. It destroyed only dirt and vegetation in most cases. Because such fire preparation was normal we grunts could not easily determine when an LZ was "hot" or actively defended. As the choppers went into the LZ they often did not touch down so we jumped, sometimes as high as several feet or more above the ground, especially into tall elephant grass. If the chopper touched down it was only for an instant as the grunts, some already standing on the skids, piled off. The infantrymen fanned out to protect the LZ until the entire element had been landed. LZs were seldom hot and I do not recall an assault into a hot LZ. Sometimes they were so small I was amazed a chopper could get us in or out. The pilots pushed their aircraft to the limits of capability and beyond.

Photo opportunities abounded while seated on the floors edge of an open-doored "Huey", legs hanging in the wind.

Pilot Potential

I had hoped to attend helicopter flight school myself in 1966. As the United States deepened its combat role in Vietnam, the army expanded its Warrant Officer program for helicopter pilots. My buddy from infantry training and jump school, Freddie Robbins, and I were stationed in the same rifle company in the 101st Airborne at Ft. Campbell – B Company, 1st Battalion, 506th Infantry. We agreed that a future in the infantry held little promise, whereas rotary wing pilot qualifications would have civilian application. We applied for the program and after many weeks of working around our training schedules and using our off-duty time for several physical and aptitude tests, we were accepted.

"Saunders – First Cav"! Wondrous apprehension hiked up my heartrate at a February pre-dawn company formation. First Sergeant Rose tolled my name for transfer to Vietnam. Robbins was on the same list. We were to be infantrymen in the First Cavalry Division, the "Cav," in Vietnam. It had a reputation. One brigade, or one-third of the infantry complement of the Cav, were paratroopers. Before the Cav deployed to Vietnam in the summer of 1965, many from the 101st filled its ranks. The First Cav slugged it out toe to toe with the North Vietnamese in the Ia Drang Valley in November and remained in action. It was the hot unit. We "cherry" troopers followed it attentively in the news. Many of its casualties were buddies of the old timers in our outfit. Those of us slated for the Cav felt a sense of being both destined for and condemned to hard service, but also grand adventure. Or, was I to be a fly boy?

Officially Robbins and I awaited deployment to Vietnam with that massive infantry replacement levy that snagged virtually all our buddies from jump school and other troopers throughout the 101st Airborne. That division seemed a transient assignment for men either going to Vietnam, or coming from there to finish out their hitch. Division headquarters informed us, however, that we would soon receive orders to attend flight school, which would cancel our orders for Vietnam. Robbins got his orders for flight school, but I heard nothing. My departure date for a leave prior to travel to Vietnam came, so I left Ft. Campbell. I was perplexed, but that was the army way. One cannot apply logic or reason to explain the mysteries of institutional machinations.

One year later, the day before I left Vietnam, I met an acquaintance – also named Saunders – from my former company at Ft. Campbell. He mentioned that my helicopter test scores and related data were located in his personnel file. The first letter of his given name preceded mine in the alphabet. A personnel clerk at Ft. Campbell had placed my flight school test scores into the first "Saunders" file in the drawer. The clerical fumble fated me for a dog's perspective of Vietnam. I had hoped for an eagle's view. At the time of the revelation I was sliding into home plate and did not care. But many times during that year in Vietnam I had envied those pilots and their dry feet. I had also saluted their courage.

What is my response to the sound of chopper blades whacking the air today? An adrenaline surge – a harbinger of dread and danger, or rest and rescue – livens my nerves. It is incongruous that almost 40 years later my daughter, Amanda, pilots a Huey.

6

FIGHTING SOLDIERS

Hard Service

Army and Marine combat infantry – probably less than ten percent of those who served in Vietnam – bore the brunt of the ground war. The other military branches supported the infantry. Even in an infantry unit, many persons were assigned to headquarters or in various rear area support tasks and, therefore, had little or no involvement in actual combat operations. Infantry grunts did the fighting, hard work and suffering and –for the most part – sustained the losses. Official casualty records tell only a partial story. Common ailments like jungle rot, ringworm and intestinal disorders eventually cleared up after we got home. I suspect that many who contracted malaria, hepatitis, amoebic dysentery and other of the myriad serious diseases available in Vietnam had long-term adverse health consequences. The maladies mattered little to them at the time – most were happy for a hospital reprieve from field operations. The enterprise of ground combat itself had emotional effects with which many failed to successfully cope. And for those who have, the experience sometimes dulls life's luster and, at other times, burnishes it.

Being a combat soldier is a point of pride. At his country's call he has the hardest and most dangerous job on the planet. He develops a resentment with tones of jealousy towards those servicemen who do not share the hardship and danger. In later life that outlook evolves for some into personal isolation of various degrees as it relates to civilians. A huge number of Americans served in Vietnam. A small percentage of those actually fought in the Vietnam War. The army with renowned impersonal unfairness treated all soldiers the same. For example, a clerk with a soft safe office job, perhaps air-conditioned, slept each night uninterrupted in a clean dry bed. The length of his tour of duty, one year, was the same as for the infantry, and he received R & R just like the infantryman.

I recall several times when our rifle platoon or company – fresh out of the bush – moved through a division forward area, or were enroute from the "golf course" helipad and airstrip to our company base area at Camp Radcliff. Some non-combat rear-area personnel considered these places dangerous. But danger is relative, and to grunts such places felt as safe and secure as the back porch. These guys eyed us with awe or perhaps pity, for our unwashed bodies were foul and our appearance was disheveled and hunched with weapons and ordnance. They never smarted off, and made way in silence for us to pass. We were wild-eyed trail-hardened drovers in Dodge City for a spree.

Our attitude became tribal, so extreme that we had little more regard for the "clerks and jerks in the rear with the gear" than for the enemy. Shortly after I arrived there, our unit returned to Camp Radcliff from operation Crazy Horse for a few days to rest and refit. That night the low-ceiling beer shack next to our company area was jammed with GIs drinking warm beer. There was no ice. Everyone got drunk and had to sleep with weapons at hand and haltered in gear because we were on alert. Late in the night mortar or rocket fire crumped in the distance. We wobbled – loaded for bear – into the defilade of the creek bed behind our squad tents. The aiming point of the enemy fire was the "golf course" and all the rounds impacted far away in that vicinity. We drunks cheered each explosion, perversely delighted and entertained because the rear area people were targeted.

A Choice

    I had a choice. Mike Lewellen had worked for a while as company clerk and the First Sergeant liked him. The tour of the regular clerk was at end, and "Top" asked Lewellen for a recommendation for a clerk replacement. It required the ability to type and spell, and some common sense. Lewellen and I were good buddies and he asked if I wanted the job. The real question was: "Did I want to live cleanly and safely in the rear area and sleep all night every night on a cot in a dry place?" I declined for inexpressible reasons. It sets well with me now, but I had many regrets thereafter in Vietnam.

    An intelligent recent replacement in 3rd platoon named McGowan was personable and could type. I suggested him. He was absolutely delighted! In McGowan's eyes I walked on water. He became a well-placed clerk at battalion headquarters and he kept me posted on rear area matters, such as the name of the captain who stole my souvenir ChiCom SKS rifle. When I saw him the day before I went home he offered to "age" me. I would be home a few days before my 20th birthday. In Wisconsin you were supposed to be 21 to enjoy "what made Milwaukee famous." McGowan made me a new genuine military ID card and rolled my birth date back one year.

    Mike Lewellen and his mortar platoon buddy, Chuck Maguire, were hard-core combat soldiers. They were teamed up at basic, then for infantry training, also in jump school and during their combat tour of duty with the Cav in Vietnam. They returned to the States, became jumpmasters, and volunteered to return to the war together as infantry NCO's in the 101st Airborne. Both sustained serious wounds, but recovered.

7
LIFESTYLES

Fauna

Everything in Vietnam either shoots, explodes, bites, cuts, chills, infects, poisons, itches, rots, exhausts, parches, burns or stabs. Vietnam is a land of alien plants and creatures in an environment strange and unhealthy to boys from the midwest. Dragonfly-sized mosquitoes – as numerous as bacteria – thirsted for American blood. Insect repellent was as essential as free cigarettes and regular mail to maintaining GI morale. At first mosquito bites swelled my face and eyes. Eventually, I became accustomed to their torment. The majority of grunts initially sent to Vietnam contracted malaria. By the time I arrived there troops were required to take a weekly malaria pill and, because of the particularly virulent strain of malaria in our area, an additional weekly pill. It seemed that half of the members of our platoon were evacuated for malaria anyway. The more severe cases were sent to hospitals in Japan. To reduce high fever, patients were placed in an alcohol and ice bath under a fan. Nonetheless, they welcomed any respite from field duty.

In the jungle I saw large and strange looking insects. Centipedes were common. Some were larger than your middle finger – and poisonous. A man in our platoon was bitten by one in the face, swelling his entire head. Scorpions of all colors and sizes were also commonplace. Their sting was not serious or fatal, but was quite painful. Just before my flight home, I opened a manila folder containing my orders and looked in. A small black scorpion scuttled out.

Fire ants were a bane. Colonies of them in overhanging vegetation, enraged by your disturbance, dropped onto your neck and swarmed in to inflict fiery bites. Burdened and cinched with gear, the GI had no defense. Army ants were fascinating. Millions of them marched unstoppable through the jungle in endless ribbons. These invaders crossed creeks via overarching vegetation or by forming a live ant ball and floating over. More than once I rapidly surrendered my sleeping spot to their relentless drive. My ears heard their crinkling-like approach, warning that I lay directly in their path.

The peasant rice farmers worked the land biblical style. Water buffalo (their beasts of burden) were not only invaluable assets, they were also pets. These large animals appeared docile and timid when handled by the Vietnamese. I marveled to see small children herding huge buffalo with a light bamboo switch. The beasts were not so friendly to GIs, however, and would occasionally charge Americans. There was no choice but to shoot them. It was anguishing to hear the poor peasants wailing over their dead buffalo. One black night on patrol in a deep dry canal bed, I walked directly behind the patrol leader, Gervase. We could see virtually nothing. Each man held onto the suspenders of the man ahead. Gervase's M-16 rifle pointed straight ahead with the safety off, finger on the trigger, so that if the barrel touched anything, he fired. After we proceeded for a time slowly and silently in this manner, his M-16 erupted. The barrel contacted the head of a water buffalo standing in the canal. It dropped on the spot.

Hobbled

Vietnamese peasants were genuine organic farmers and recycling was their way of life. Their simple dwellings lacked power or plumbing. They had no outhouses but answered nature's

Peasants harvest rice near Ft. Lonely.

Tricycle chassis Labrettas provided peasants with "modern" transport. Bicycles cargoed with clay pots were more common.

call in their stagnant rice paddies – receptacles for all waste, animal and human.

One day a sharp long thorn poked through the canvas side of my jungle boot into my ankle joint and broke off. I removed it, but we were soon plodding calf deep in rice paddy filth. Within only a few hours the ankle swelled from raging infection. Our platoon was on the move for several days. Even with buddies carrying much of my gear, walking for any distance and keeping pace seemed impossible. Doc tagged me for medevac, but no choppers came in that day. He injected two needles of penicillin into me. Months earlier I had found that the literal meaning of "can't" seldom really applies. The next day using my M-16 for a crutch, I hobbled with pain and difficulty and somehow kept up, simply because I had to. The day was miserable and anticipation of another one was worrisome. The penicillin, however, had taken hold and during the night the infection subsided. The next day it died as quickly as it had grown.

For much of the year the rice paddies remain flooded or soupy. Often the only passage is by elevated trails routing through them or atop narrow hard packed dikes which divide the fields and control the water levels. A man walking ahead of me in file stepped from the trail and sunk to his knees in paddy mud. The more he stomped to extricate himself, the deeper he went. At stomach level he still had not found bottom. After six of us yanked on him from the bank, the muck finally released him to duty. Everyone was cracking up. Then our point element drew fire. It choked the levity.

Reptiles

A lizard species was the mouthpiece for Vietnam. To my astonishment during watch on my first night in the field, I heard from the bush "fuck you" again and again in a computer-voice-like intonation. It was the infamous "fuck you" lizard and his unusual call, welcoming me to his homeland. Had he met SSgt. Saltzman on the bus at Ft. Knox?

Snakes were ever-present. During the monsoon season they were always visible swimming in the low areas and flooded rice paddies. When walking in or near thick bamboo you could see and hear snakes scuttling away through the thickets. Leaning against the wall of a sandbag bunker talking to my buddy, I heard a noise beside my head among cardboard M-60 bandoliers like mice in the cupboard. Rogers told me to freeze and I did. It was a "two step turn," a small lime green krait – a highly poisonous viper – beside my head. Its moniker described the bite's lethality for the victim who, it was said, would take two steps, turn around and drop dead. Amazingly, I know of only a couple of men bitten by snakes.

In the jungle lurked long large constrictor snakes. They hung silent and stiff from the banyan trees. Some trees bore scratches and scars high off the ground. They were tiger scratching posts. Monkeys howled. Exotic creatures hooted and chattered. The thick green multi-layered jungle canopy shed sunlight and caged rot.

On one occasion our patrol rested momentarily in a bamboo thicket facing one another on opposite sides of a tiny clearing. We sat leaning back upon our rucksacks. Just then a long brown-banded snake slithered between the rows of boots and decided to turn into the bamboo where I sat. It came straight at me. I attempted to back up and slid back, pack and all, as fast as I could, but the snake was much faster. Then it paused and feigned a couple of strikes at my crotch. I rolled to the side in alarm and we both escaped. My buddies laughed.

The Vietnamese ate snakes. Occasionally we were located in the vicinity of South Vietnamese Popular Force Units, a militia. They looked comical in oversized WWII American helmets and armament. It took two of them to carry a BAR, an automatic rifle. Their tactical discipline was like Girl Scouts on a campout and their military effectiveness was no better. A few times a large volume of small arms fire came from their direction. Soon they paraded by with no ammo, but proudly displayed one or more large snakes destined for the cook pot. They had expended a basic load of ammo for the delicacy.

Blood Suckers

Leeches were overabundant in jungle and highland jungle areas, especially during the monsoon season when nothing ever dried out – not the terrain, our clothes, or our skin. These dark brown, wormy, slimy blood suckers thrived on the wet ground and in the water. When a leech sensed human body heat, it ambled towards the source with a determined inch-worm movement. As GI's moved down a trail, leeches, sensing body heat from the first man passing by, rose upright swaying their ugly business end ready to latch onto the next man's jungle boots and then head north. The tops of our socks were usually stiff with dry blood. Leeches sated with ankle blood burst in the socks. Tucking the jungle pant legs into your boots provided insufficient defense. When you sleep and live on the earth you are just another co-equal creature. I have seen leeches on virtually every part of the body. I once woke with one securely fastened between my eye and the bridge of my nose. A buddy of mine had one on his eyelid. The warmest body regions got their most devoted attention. Everyone heard the rumor of a man who had a small one crawl up inside his penis.

Leeches are all sizes. A fat one adhering to my upper ankle was so long it wrapped its body all the way around it. Once fastened, the critters could not be easily pulled off. Application of salt or a burning cigarette eventually dropped them. The noxious GI mosquito repellent was an effective leech killer. It instantly curled them in agony. Leech saliva contains an anesthetic, so their auger through skin and blood suction had no sting or bite. Often you did not sense their presence until they had had a good meal. Rumor had it that a soldier from the 173rd Airborne Brigade pinned down in a rice paddy had lost so much blood to leeches that he needed a transfusion. Not believable, but illustrative.

We never wanted for munitions or cigarettes, but in the earlier part of my tour we had difficulty getting most comfort items, such as dry socks, or the newly issued jungle fatigues and jungle boots. These items did not filter down to the grunts who really needed them until all of the rear area army and air force troops were outfitted and the excess seeped through the system to the needy. The old style fatigues were made of heavy cotton and had few and impractical pockets. Robbins' (not Freddie) old fatigues were rotten. On one day's "hump" a leg of his pants ripped off. For days he trudged highland jungle with only one pant leg. My friend, Bruce "Doc" Hartnell (the platoon medic), and I were chatting side by side when Robbins approached in his tattered pants and said "Doc, you've got to do something – my guts are coming out of my asshole." Hartnell told him to bend over. To our amusement, there were about six large fat happy leeches fastened to Robbins' anus. Doc administered a squirt of mosquito repellent, an instant remedy, and gave Robbins a gauze to self apply. It was hilarious.

8

MY YOUNG FRIEND

Village Boy

    Infantry combat is man's most extreme experience. It demands a suppression of one's natural compassion, so that you can look almost undistressed and without tears at appalling scenes, but you hear haunting sounds that echo down the years. These images become very painful and they change you.

    Only parts of the following episode peer through the fog of my memory, but the sound remains clear and everlasting. Our unit had made several helicopter air assaults earlier that day. Where or why is a bewildering blur. I remember my platoon, 3rd platoon, lined up assaulting through an enemy bunker/trench system located in a small hamlet, firing as we advanced. I recall no return fire. For the first time I saw a freshly dead NVA, his body hunched next to a spider hole littered with ammunition magazines and expended shell casings. The rain had washed away the blood, exposing his brain clean and waxy like the model in biology class.

    Later in the day we retraced our advance and then waited at the edge of the village near a rice paddy for the choppers to extract our unit. While walking through the village a young boy of 6-8 years came up beside me and we bantered and joked back and forth without language. In the center of the village we passed by a large thatched hooch which hummed from the chatter of women and crying young children, crowded in there sheltered from the firing and the rain.

The boy and I sat on the dike near the rice paddy, sharing my favorite C-ration snack, mixed jam and peanut butter on crackers. Then I gave him a tropical chocolate bar, chewing gum and cigarettes. He stayed around and I had ideas of taking him with us, away from an uncertain future, but that was impossible.

White Phosphorous

Small H-13 two-man observation helicopters supported our combat sweep through the area that day. They hovered and circled low above us, pointing out bunkers, marking potential targets with smoke grenades or attacking some directly by dropping white phosphorous grenades on them. These brave men were easy targets themselves. Overhead nearby a pilot was shot in the foot. He landed the chopper just behind us and our medic treated the wound. The aviator immediately remounted his machine and continued his mission.

Third platoon waited for the helicopter airlift as we relaxed and ate at the edge of the village. The observation choppers continued to circle and search the area. Then abruptly and inexplicably, the helicopter gunner/observers dropped white phosphorous grenades on many of the hooches. The choppers hovered directly above each hooch, dropped a grenade in through the thatched roof and proceeded to the next one to do the same. White phosphorous, the substance of some hand grenades, mortars and artillery shells, makes a horrible weapon. Its white billowy explosion launches cascading orange clumps of smoldering phosphorous material that burns as long as air fuels it. It sears through flesh. Why the helicopter crews grenaded after the ground action had ceased is only one of those thousand bewilderments of war.

Tragedy

The following can only be blamed on communication screw-up of the worst sort. The haven of those women and children became their death trap. White phosphorous grenades dropped directly onto their hooch. Their piercing screams stabbed through my ears down into my heart. Paszkiewitz and I poised to ready the M-60 machine gun to shoot down the chopper, but it was a belated empty gesture; we could not have made ourselves do it anyway. The helicopter crews knew not what they did. Sickened and saddened beyond words, I thought of those burned children throughout the years and I remember the boy to whom I was so drawn. How that day changed his world! Surely he had family there. He was near when the screams knifed into us. For an everlasting moment our eyes locked as the horrid shrieks branded our spirits. His eyes transformed from young to old in that instant. Then he looked away and trod from the village, across the paddies towards the surrounding hills. How could he understand? How could I understand? I am sure he joined the VC. Sometimes my mind forgets not to remember.

9

GALLOWS HUMOR

It is called the *Infan*try for good reason. Except for career NCOs, the common age in our platoon was 19 or 20. We called Davis, a 24-year-old private, "gramps." My 19th birthday was soon after I arrived there. Some guys in the company were younger. One was 16. The first 17-year-old American KIA in Vietnam was in our company, killed long before I arrived there. Our teenage capacity for fun and frolic had few bounds. We never missed an opportunity for comic relief and grab ass. Subconsciously we celebrated being alive and intact. I treasured up the texture of life in the moment. I felt more alive there.

Bad food tasted better there than good food did later. Humor was easier then. We wrung it from any event and every situation, however unlikely or normally inappropriate. Basic first aid for prevention of shock, among other things, is not to allow the injured person to view his wound and to reassure him. When Doc Hartnell was seriously wounded, Robbins told him: "Gee Doc, it looks real bad." Then Robbins was squeamish to stick Doc with morphine, so Doc drafted Lewellen to slap the syrette into his thigh. We laughed and wise cracked about Robbins' quip ever afterward.

Horseplay

In Tuy Hoa members of C Company's mortar platoon found several ponies and horses, some with raw backs. The VC had used them for transport so the mortar platoon used the healthy ones for awhile to carry its tubes, base plates and ammunition. When a tall mare came into season, the availability of her charms was much appreciated by a short-legged pony stallion. But no matter how hard he pressed his suit, his legs were too short to obtain the position necessary to sate his ardor. Admiring his persistence, GIs dispensed "Love Potion Number Nine." They deepened a shallow in the ground and led in the mare. There she stood in grateful accommodation to the short stud who, true to military maxim, occupied the high ground and penetrated the objective, serenaded by the lusty cheers of grimy GIs.

Rude Awakening

One night during the spring of 1967 I was assigned two men and ordered to establish an observation post/ambush on a three-way trail junction, a two hour walk into the valley below our highland fire base, LZ Santana. That I was able to locate the exact position was miraculous, given my poor navigational skill, but we three were in position by dark. It was an exposed and dangerous place too far from help. A faint deep throated "bloop" met our ears. In a few seconds a shell exploded 20 feet on the opposite side of the raised trail, which also served as a rice paddy dike. Then two more erupted in rapid deafening intervals. It was "H and I," harassment and interdiction, fire from our battalion's powerful 4.2 inch mortars located at the fire base. These rounds were intended to, by pure chance, kill any enemy who just happened to be there. The three of us were not dug in. The battalion fire direction center, of course, knew where we were, but nonetheless had plotted the fire so dangerously close. I was furious. Shrapnel flew low overhead while we flattened on our bellies. A kneeling man would have been cut in half. Without the fortuitous protection of the paddy dike, the mortar fire would have killed us.

Absolute silence was essential. The night was cloudy and totally dark. The mortars quit and we began watch, one man awake, two sleeping. Suddenly a loud stream of cursing broke the black silence. What? It had been too dark to move about, so Adams – the man on watch, having to urinate merely stood up and let it fly – right on the sleeping man's face. At the time I thought this was the funniest thing that I ever knew, even though we all remained alert for the remainder of the night. It passed quietly.

Acrobatics

On another night our platoon was moving single file with disciplined silence, intending to attack an enemy position in the darkness. My machine gun team was the rear element. The assistant gunner, John Barra, was behind me. The platoon had crossed a wide deep canal on a plank. Immediately after I was over, Barra lost balance, began to fall and made a hilarious "ah-ah-ah-ah" sound as he tilted. His arms, trying to flail to catch his balance, were impeded by a can of machine gun ammo in each hand as he plopped on his back into one foot of filthy yellowed muck on the canal bottom – still clutching the ammo. We spectators laughed uncontrollably.

Dunk

One evening a few days later, I moved out on patrol with the gun carried horizontally across my right shoulder as usual. Just outside our perimeter a part of the trail served as the lip of a small but deep foul farm pond. When I walked by the pond the trail bank collapsed under me into the pond and I sank all the way. They said it looked like only my cap and machine gun were boating at the regatta. The bottom muck clutched my boots. The man behind deftly plucked out the gun by the top carrying handle and then me. The boys gave me a big hand. I countered that the drenching relieved any anxiety about the dreaded, inevitable rain to fall in the night. They, on the other hand, would speculate and fret about it and how to stay dry. I relaxed, contented in my discomfort. The joke was on me. The night sky remained starlit and dry.

POW

Sergeant First Class Juan Jose was a short native Hawaiian who resembled the Vietnamese. As a lark once, I took him as a prisoner of war. The idea was to fake out the company headquarters element. Jose removed his GI gear and clothing, slipped on a pair of Ho Chi Minh sandals cut from old tires – standard footgear for the NVA – and placed a conical straw peasant hat on his head. I trained a rifle on him and marched him into the company headquarters area. They tied a POW tag on him and prepared him for evacuation before we broke the joke.

Third platoon sergeant, Hawaiian SFC Juan Jose, posed as an enemy POW.

Deadeye

A 3rd platoon squad once surprised five NVA at breakfast and immediately shot four of them at close range. One was hit in the thigh and quickly doubled over. My buddy thought the NVA had a grenade so he fired a 20 round magazine directly at him.

After the dust cleared the guys discovered that the "crackshot" had only shot off the NVA's earlobe. We teased him about his marksmanship for several weeks thereafter.

Stump

A tone of absurdity edged with cynicism garnished our gallows humor and mischief. We never moved to a final night ambush position during daylight. Instead we assembled close by at dusk. To conceal the location of the trap we waited until dark to move in. One ambush assembly area was littered with NVA bodies. I sat down among them on the sandy ground and leaned back on my pack. Butch walked over. He spied a handy seat. His rifle butt rested on the ground. He shifted weight to it and lowered. In the dusky gloaming he had seen a small tree stump. I knew better. So did others nearby. It was the doubled leg of a dead NVA. The flesh was black with death. The knee was the top. Doubled calf and thigh formed the trunk. It stood upright in the sand – its base the buried corpse. Butch cut power. My leg bent up, poised. Butch's ass descended. I coiled my leg. Butch's tail came down inches to contact – inches from corrupted mush. My leg struck out. My jungle boot fanged his ass. He tumbled onto the ground. It was burlesque. We laughed – from the belly. So did Butch. Maybe you had to be there.

Sewer Plant

What follows is so absurd it is humorous. The pervading smell of the rear area was that of burning shit, literally. For sanitary reasons, burning was the method of human waste disposal. At Camp Radcliff, the base of the First Cavalry Division and thousands of men, the latrines were multi-holer screened shacks built upon concrete pads. The rear and lower portion of the shack was hinged, and halved 55 gallon drums were slid under each hole. When filled and teeming with thousands of maggots, the drums were dragged out by hand, diesel or aviation fuel added, and the mix was stirred and ignited. After several hours of adding fuel, mixing and burning, the tantalizing treasure went up in black befouled smoke. It had to be the worst job on earth. This was rock bottom; any bounce would at least be elevating. Some wore gas masks when performing the chore. Remember that the temperature was in the 90's and 100's – humidity as high – and the drums always overflowed. They had no handles. As you dragged this heavy filth on the rough concrete it slopped and slobbered over and down your hands. It took several hours of adding fuel and constantly stirring the mixture to burn off the liquids. I did this three times when I first arrived in country.

The procedure was called "burning the shithouse." One new trooper was ordered to "burn the officer's shithouse" and he, new to the concept, carried out his orders literally – burning it to the ground. My war was a carnival of the preposterous. Burning the shithouse was the most disgusting chore that I ever performed. Truly a "shit" detail. The thick and odious pervading smell of burning crap, urine, maggots and diesel fuel is my enduring impression of Camp Radcliff. And it is the scent of humility.

10

LIVING CONDITIONS

Sleep

The sheer physical misery and exhaustion we withstood is not shown in photos or film. It can only be truly known by enduring it. Living on the ground out in the weather is harsh even for young healthy men. The adverse effects are cumulative.

I adapted to sleep anywhere under any conditions. I have slid and slept on muddy slopes, bedded down with crawly critters on the jungle floor, bunked in driving rain and deep puddles, and slumbered beside squealing bunker rats that tracked across my neck. So long as my face was covered from direct rain, I could readily snooze. Except for thirst, want of sleep is the body's most urgent craving. We never had enough, and often sleep was not refreshing. Usually we maintained two-man positions around a nighttime perimeter defense. One man at each position remained on watch during the night. So at best one slept only half of the night, unless he was on night patrol or ambush when he got little or no sleep.

As soon as my eyelids closed I was out. Mr. Sandman and I scuffled and skirmished during my watches. I could trick him usually. I sang all of the oldies in my head, tallied shooting stars, counted from 1000 backwards, brewed hot chocolate on the foxhole floor, but dozed sometimes anyway – if only for moments. Sleep always stalked in the shadows. Sometimes I slept upright with my eyes open – mind asleep, body awake and vice versa. Often I sat on my helmet so that a snoozing tilt would tip me over. One morning I woke up, having slept the night through with no watch duty. Four of us were in that position and I blamed the previous watch for falling asleep and not waking me. Not so. He and two others tried to wake me for my watch to no avail. They shook and shook me and even rolled me over, but I remained catatonic.

During a night of incessant monsoon rain it was discovered that every man in 3rd platoon was asleep, even though we had the most advanced and exposed placement of C Company. Unless an enemy threat was apparent and imminent, it was natural to become lax – even in our unit in which discipline was so strict.

Lt. Collins caught my friend, PFC Randy Pierson, sleeping on guard. Collins said nothing, but took Pierson's M-16 rifle. When Pierson woke at dawn he imagined that the enemy had infiltrated and pilfered the weapon, but he soon learned its whereabouts. Collins lashed Pierson fiercely with his tongue and then sold the M-16 back to him for $300, a just and appropriate sanction. These few instances of carelessness on guard are specifically recalled only because they were so infrequent. Sleeping on guard was serious, seldom and never deliberate.

When I was a fresh replacement, Pierson tried to con me about guard watch. I nudged him for first call about five minutes before his watch time. He refused to budge and kept snoozing for another 15-20 minutes into my sleep time. This pattern continued for two or three nights until I solved it. I gave him the first call a full half hour before his watch was to begin. After his usual extra half-hour bag act and long wake-up he was right on schedule. He cussed me out, but after that he got up when I first shook him.

Randy and I became fast friends after that. Driving back to my apartment near Ft. Campbell, Kentucky a year later, I recognized the gait of a GI walking along the road. It was Pierson. I took him home to meet my wife, Denise, and eat a steak. Pierson and I got very drunk that night.

Intruder

Critters prowl at night. Claymores are deadly antipersonnel mines jammed with hundreds of ball bearings, placed above ground facing the enemy. They are hand detonated via a power cord connected to a hand igniter. Rogers and I placed one 15 yards ahead of our machine gun on a trail through dense elephant grass. The next morning it was turned around pointing in our faces. Often we booby trapped them with hand grenades or trip flares by pulling the pin and deftly placing the grenade beneath the claymore. If disturbed, the claymore eased the tension on the release lever or "spoon" of the flare or grenade and it ignited or exploded. The VC were known to steal both the grenade and the claymore mine.

Skin Rot

The Asian monsoon is relentless. We were usually wet and often soaked. Whenever we dried out – giving us a rotten-dishrag pissed-pants smell – it would rain again, or we waded a creek or plopped through a flooded paddy. Pruny skin is only medium wetness. For instance, it rained or drizzled almost every moment of a seven-day three-man long-range outpost which I led in early 1967. Our skin deteriorated from pruny to waterlogged – like sopping wallpaper. When you scratched yourself, both the itch and the skin peeled off under your grubby nails.

My foxhole buddy, Pierson, and I once made a deal to take turns airing our feet. To do so simultaneously was unbearably nauseating even with our hardened noses. Constant immersion rapidly turned feet yellowish-green and pitted the calluses. Several days in that condition caused socks to adhere to the skin. Foot casualties were commonplace. One tall kid had half-dollar sized cankers on the tops of both feet and cut out the boot tops so he could walk. He was not evacuated – not even close. You had to be bleeding or spike a 102° temperature in order to be taken out. Three clear sunny days in mid-January lifted our soggy spirits and saggy morale after twenty-nine straight days and nights of rain.

Jungle rot was a bane. Laundry and bathing were rare. We fermented in our own crud. Filth and moisture combined to create oozy skin boils, or raw open blotches, or cankers. Some men were seriously affected. My crotch was raw and oozing for the entire year. Elsewhere puss boils bothered me. It took months after I returned to the States before my skin cleared. An ever enlarging patch of ringworm blighted my lower leg. It took a year to grow and a year to heal.

Bennie's Warmth

The temperature in Vietnam was not always tropical, for in the highlands it could drop as low as the 50's at night. Pleasant enough unless you are wet, and then there is the wind. We chilled for weeks clad only in our thin jungle fatigues. Our scrounger, Bennie Holbrook, appeared one day at a brigade forward base with a box of wool GI sweaters, enough for each of us. Their origin remained a mystery. Anything owned by the U.S. government was rightfully ours, we thought. We were tribal and it was immaterial if gear belonged to another clan. Nuggets of comfort like sweaters were scarce as snake horns. Somewhere in the long chain of supply, light fingers filched a link. Grunts could not rely on the army to timely satisfy basic clothing needs – socks, sweaters, and boots. You had to either wait or buy them on the black market. The dilemma: you needed the item *now*, and the store was open only to city folks.

I still hear Bennie's mischievous prideful chuckle and see that toothless gap in his grin as he doled out the loot. He had pilfered from a rear area hoard. Palaver and piracy were his forté. His joking yarns of teen antics back on the block entertained us by the hour. The main subjects – adventures at his girlfriend's house and other delinquencies. Bennie did not long despair when the inevitable "Dear John" arrived. But the target of his glib darts switched from army chicken shit and other current events to the "bitch and her stud."

His playful sense of humor graced the world for only 18 years. He slept for another five. Frags from a booby trap grenade violated his brain. He was, I heard, lucid before surgery at Walter Reed Army Hospital – but he never woke up. In 1989 Bennie's father, his namesake, told me that Bennie lay in a coma until he died in 1972.

Cold Ambush

The coldest night happened during an ambush. Tom Dougher and I shared one of several trailside positions along the kill zone. After we settled in, the dark sky opened. It was as if the individual drops waited and accumulated before plunging at once upon us like an airborne river. Then the wind lashed buckets of piercing water at us. Ponchos were forbidden on ambush. Their noise and shine were too revealing. In the black of night and the clamor of the storm, any prey escaped the ambush unseen and unheard. Dougher and I sat leaning on each other back to back in a futile attempt to glean each other's body heat. We shivered incessantly in the numbing cold. Dougher vomited from the shaking and then dry heaves racked him. How many thousands of insignificant individual routine instances of such sufferings are unchronicled, which just hang in time?

11

THIRST

Cravings

Most people have not learned to appreciate water. I mean not only cold water gorging over your tongue and pooling a sated coolness in the belly. I mean fetid scummy water. I mean anything to slake a thirst so imploring that it focuses your mind and body to the exclusion of all other impulse – except how to get a swig of it to suck through your cracked lips. In the early part of my tour we did some hard humping in the highland jungle, day after day. At first I was not physically hardened to it, deficient in mental toughness and resignation to a dire situation. That changed, but not enough.

The heat and humidity conspired with the tonnage toted on my body to incite the strongest craving ever to come into me. The physical demands of movement up, down, and through the backbreaking terrain were none like I had experienced or imagined. You could not quit – and Indians scalped stragglers. It was so oppressive that sweat dripped steadily from the cuff of my soaked fatigue jacket. You could down nearly a quart GI canteen in one good suck, but you dared not. Our path may cross a stream soon enough to refill, or it may not. I silently thanked my high school football coach for banning all water from our summer three-hour practices. Still, there was a harsh adjustment to make. I just could not get enough water and, like others, fixated on the dilemma. At my request my parents mailed a three-quart metal canteen. Eventually, I acquired four GI canteens. You could not carry enough water for satisfaction. The only solution was to adjust your attitude.

Thirst and fatigue fostered an ambivalence to danger and threat. The normal concern for enemy contact or booby traps often succumbed to a competing desire for rest and water of any quality.

Secretly I hoped the enemy would hit us – just so I could lay down for awhile. Village wells often yielded foul, gray, cloudy water – probably from laundering. Stagnant buffalo wallow pools and ground depressions were always foul with slime or iridescent scum. We did not care; just pop in two iodine tablets per canteen. Thirst overcomes foul taste.

Refills

Any opportunity to top off our canteens was not to be ignored. At mid-day during a long- range patrol we passed a shallow depression in a bone-dry rice paddy. A few inches of stagnant and reeking scum-coated water languished in the bottom of this buffalo wallow, evaporating under the blazing sun. SSgt. Thomopolous, our leader, forbid us to fill our canteens. The water was not "moving" and we should encounter a good source before long, he reasoned.

Pierson and I took no chances. We could always dump our canteens if we found better water. We hung back and Pierson wiggled his boot in the slime. He said, "See it move." We filled up. The patrol ran across no other water sources that day. The men were seriously parched when we stopped for the night. Pierson and I shared with the others, except Thomopolous. We commented that he could not drink it anyway because it was not "moving." He was too proud to ask for a swallow.

Our party beverage was "rabbit," water mixed in a helmet with kool aid packets enclosed in mail from home, the same helmet used to shave and launder socks. To this day my mind holds a Vietnam angle on water. I delight in a cool drink, it is the most lasting physical appreciation which I gained from there.

Hill Disaster

One oppressively hot sunny day during the dry season, C Company, having been on the move for days, was due for resupply. Probably company headquarters was informed at the last minute. Anyway, the company was located in a low area of largely bamboo tangle, an impossible LZ for the resupply helicopters. The company was ordered to climb to a nearby hill, the crown of which would be a suitable place to land helicopters. The hill was a substantial height and very steep, devoid of any trail or convenient avenue leading to the summit. Moreover, 6-10 foot tall stiff, sharp-bladed elephant grass guarded the slopes like silent sentinels. It encased the heat and humidity and shielded the hill from any breeze. It grew so thick in places you had to face away and lay back into it to bust a path. I heard that the company commander told his superior that if C Company ascended that hill he would have no company left at the top.

C Company began the climb in a column of several single files of men. I carried the M-60, some ammo and my usual cargo. Pierson, the assistant gunner, followed carrying a few hundred rounds in cans. Scores of other boots tread the way ahead of us so the elephant grass was flattened to the dry earth, smoothing and glazing our path. No other vegetation or handholds were present to pull ourselves uphill. The poor traction, the climb, and the climate quickly spent us and sickened many with heat exhaustion and dehydration. Men collapsed in the elephant grass beside the trail as others trudged on. My theory was to bull on ahead because suffering is most handily borne if its duration, though intensified, is shortened. I was trancelike, plodding up the hill, drenched in sweat. That god-damned gun weighed a ton; my tongue adhered to my mouth with desiccated gooey spit. I hallucinated; maybe blacked out awhile, too. Even at my tortoise pace, I was among the first group to reach the crest. I dropped my gear, peeled off my soggy shirt and held it up to the stagnant air, just enough that it provided a cooling moment when first applied to my face. I fell in a heap on my back for a few moments. By the time Pierson came along I had rejuvenated enough to join others in retracing our steps to help those who had collapsed along the way. We placed the heat casualties on ponchos and dragged them up to the LZ at the top, an absolutely exhausting task. They babbled in confusion and dementia. I saw a medic unclasp a large safety pin and shove it through the lower lip and tongue of one GI to prevent him from swallowing his tongue in delirium. Fortunately, choppers had airlifted jerry cans of water to the LZ.

Helicopters are guided into an LZ by someone on the ground marking it with a smoke grenade, the color of which verified the locale and wind conditions. Smoke grenades pop off and spew their vaporized coloring agent with a small, brief and intense flame. A Mrs. O'Leary "popped smoke" that day and just tossed it on the grassy ground, rather than first clearing some grass for a naked spot to place it. It burned the dry elephant grass like paper. Before the day was through C Company had a disaster on its hands at no enemy expense or effort. The flames spread slowly but steadily on the LZ where the grass was shorter or pressed flat. It was imperative to relocate the prostrate heat casualties to safety. A breeze came up and the flames eased into taller grass and grew to a hell-fire, threatening parched men, laden with munitions. The scene was a ferment of smoke, confusion and near panic. Heat casualties were evacuated, but those of us at or near the top retreated from the flames down a very steep and rocky dry gully. We picked our way down, clinging to roots to impede our fall, as rocks dislodged from above fell about us. In places we plunged and broke the fall as best we could, often with braking strides like a horse descending a canyon wall.

The movies show GIs in Vietnam wearing Rambo-like head scarves or bandanas. Hollywood has always failed the Vietnam War accuracy test. Hollywood is as phony as Rambo. Luckily for me we always wore helmets, unless on ambush patrol, and usually even then. This steel pot and its bulk became a handy dome on your neck, not only for protection, but storage for photos, maps and letters; a bathtub, cook pot, sign, and camp stool. Making our way down the gully, at the oft heard warning, "rock!", we hunched our heads as loose stones and rock clattered by or upon us. I glimpsed a free falling melon sized rock above becoming ever larger and in the instant when I tucked in my head it crunched the top rear of my helmet with a clunk, knocking off the helmet and momentarily stunning me. The steel pot saved me from a skull crushing. I soon got another and never complained about wearing it.

The situation looked grave as the fire approached from the flank of the gully and threatened to burn over us. I do not remember what happened after that, whether we hunkered down and it roared over or we did indeed outrun it. I recall only the desperation of the moment. Some men from 3rd platoon who had left their weapons at the top had returned down the hill to assist with heat casualties who were trapped there by the flames. They retreated further with a serious heat casualty in tow and found a stream, immersing the stricken man to lower his body temperature and save his life. The only weapon among them was a .45 pistol and one magazine of ammunition. The fire had burned over their rifles. These men spent the night there impotent against the human enemy.

Men lost equipment, ammunition and weapons, much of it destroyed in the fire. I pitied mortar platoon. It had set up its 81 mm mortar tubes and base plates in the LZ area. We could hear the mortar rounds explode as they fell victim to the flames. I lost only my helmet and gas mask; but in the evening felt a quiet pride that we still had the gun and some ammo.

For several days I had carried a secret. A can of coke lay in my pack. It awaited the perfect moment. Then I'd savor it. Pat Hayes was my foxhole buddy that night. I would share with him only. One can was not enough to pass around. My bayonet punched it open. I took a warm and zesty swig. Unsteady with exhaustion, I set it down. It tipped over on the uneven ground. I wanted to cry.

12

AT EASE

Rucks

Our patrol once discovered an NVA marijuana supply post, a small bamboo structure with thatched roof covering scores of bread-loaf-sized packages of marijuana. We burned it. Drug use was unknown in our unit when I was there. NVA often had marijuana in their rucksacks. These rucks were handier than the GI butt pack and gave the look of a veteran who had seen action. They rode higher on the back and had 3 handy exterior pockets. I soon got one and never went back to the old GI pack.

Mail

Mail, of course, was a highlight. It was our only connection to a remote and distant past. Letters from home were to morale as gasoline is to a Chevy. My family wrote regularly and my girl wrote daily. Those letters moored me to sanity and hope. Sometimes no mail reached us for more than a week, but then it was such a treat to have a whole packet of mail. Grandma Saunders addressed her letters to me at whatever military rank popped into her civilian mind. The letters addressed to "colonel" or "general" Steve Saunders drew sarcastic comments at mail call. I was accused of telling "whoppers" to the homefolks.

The mail included newspapers like *Stars & Stripes* and a box called "101 rations," which held razor blades, toilet articles, stationery, tropical chocolate, paperbacks and cartons of cigarettes. Cigarettes were as crucial as mail to good morale and the army knew it. Many times we had to bury the oversupply. Too bad the same system did not govern procurement and distribution of dry socks.

Reading was an escape. I read Kenneth Roberts' great books: *Northwest Passage, Lydia Bailey, Rabble in Arms, Arundel, Oliver Wiswell*, and *The Lively Lady*. I devoured Cornelius Ryan's *The Longest Day* sitting in thick jungle on a listening post.

Film

We saw movies occasionally, if we were perimeter guard for an artillery firebase or on standby in the rear as a ready-reaction force. Frankie Avalon/Annette Funicello beach movies and Elvis Presley films lubed already robust libidos. We watched Henry Fonda in *The Battle of the Bulge* and the *Combat* TV series starring Vic Morrow. My buddies jabbed me about Morrow's character – "Sgt. Saunders" – a buck sergeant like me. For a few days my nickname changed from "Sandy" to "Combat." Featuring war films for the warriors was so in style for the Army. By then gushes of irony had diluted the concentrate. Besides, we were starved for any entertainment. I remember sitting on my helmet in the mud, blind to the driving rain – transfixed to the makeshift screen. That memory is a fond one. I store it next to the ones where my big brother, Gary, yielded to my tag-alongs to the Sun Theatre on Saturday afternoons half a century ago. Hours of *Bonzo, Francis The Talking Mule, The Three Stooges, Abbott and Costello*, or *Johnny Mac Brown*; a box of Root Beer Barrels chased with a Holloway sucker; feet up on the seat beside my brother – can it get any better!

Props

The national media once dramatized 3rd platoon, but we faked the scene. On Easter 1967 a noted ABC TV newsman, Frank McGee, reported a human-interest feature about our battalion Catholic chaplin. We had never set eyes on the padre until he, McGee, and attending film entourage helicoptered in that Sunday.

A combat chaplin item became the media make-believe of the moment. A cameraman directed us to stand relaxed in the background displaying weapons and gear. Then the priest and a few of 3rd platoon members posing as escort moved a short distance into the bush. The cameras rolled and the star of the fraudulent film entered the stage as if returning from the pretend patrol. Frank McGee interviewed him about war with the grunts. Another slice of infantry life. The fighters were the props while the limelight focused on the phony. The news retinue and the good father departed on the waiting helicopter. Back to the war for us.

13

ROGERS' RESCUE

In Vietnam I danced cheek to cheek with death a few times, but she smooched me only once. And it was a wet one. The army tried constantly to find and fix on the NVA and VC in order to destroy them with superior firepower and air mobility. In August of 1966 my battalion was operating in highland jungle terrain and elephant-grass savanna. In an attempt to locate an enemy force in a vast area overgrown with wild and plentiful vegetation, the battalion "checker boarded" its assigned region with small long-range recon patrols. It divided into eight-man groups, each to thoroughly search and probe its assigned sector. Only alternate terrain squares as indicated on our maps – like only the black squares on a checkerboard – were investigated by this method. In theory, the battalion could search double the total area by that method and have a reasonable probability of locating any enemy forces there. The areas to be covered by each small patrol was large enough that the mission lasted several days.

The patrol was supplied with the requisite days of C-ration meals. It was impractical to carry over 20 cans of food added to the usual 50-60 pounds of munitions and gear. I ate my fill, and stored the cans of fruit, pound cake and "B1-A unit" (snack) cans in tubes of GI socks to be secured under the pack flap and threw away the others. I had no appetite when we "humped" anyway. A can of fruit and a pound cake, and maybe a hot chocolate and a little peanut butter on crackers each day was enough. I lost 20 pounds while in Vietnam. Each day we walked endlessly looking for enemy sign. The terrain was remote and our sector revealed no sign of human habitation, only large monkeys. A former company sized NVA bivouac area was the only indication of enemy presence. This long-range patrol was but one of scores of exhausting, routine, unimportant and unremembered Vietnam ordeals – except for one event scorched into my memory.

Munitions

Each man typically carried in addition to his weapon, 400 rounds of M-16 rifle ammo or twenty-five 40mm grenades for his M-79 grenade launcher, bayonet, entrenching tool, at least two fragmentation grenades, C-rations, at least three quarts of water, poncho, poncho liner and personal items, and two or three of the following: smoke grenade, white phosphorous grenade, trip flare, parachute flare, claymore mine, or LAW (light anti-tank weapon). This freight was attached in a variety of ways to a suspender harness and pistol belt, and in a pack collectively called LBE (load bearing equipment). We did not take the machine gun on that mission. I was armed with an M-79 and carried the radio, a PRC-25 or "prick 25." The backpack FM radio was our only contact with other units, medevac and artillery support, and each patrol always carried one. It weighed about 25 pounds, plus you carried extra batteries. With the radio on your upper back the cargo was top-heavy and awkward.

Life Saved

On the second day while crossing a rock-and-boulder strewn stream raging with monsoon runoff – jumping from one rock to another – I slipped off balance. The load kept going and me with it; I sank like lead. I was probably taller than the water was deep, but the current wheeled and spun me along the bottom. I could neither stand up, nor jettison the radio and my LBE. They haltered me to the stream bed. I tried to stabilize on all fours, only to be tipped once again by the current. My panicked desperate effort to rise was futile. The flow buffeted and rolled me in the suffocating wet. My wind gave out and I was a dead man. Mind and body relaxed in complacent acceptance and I gave it up. A numb and strange sensation of well-being appeared in place of panic. I think I passed out. Then suddenly I was back, sick but sucking air.

Richard Rogers had the guts to jump into that violent angry water at the risk of his own skin, find me, and then save us both and recover my weapon. I do not know how he did it. He had been a civilian lifeguard. The patrol then continued. I recall nothing about the remainder of the mission. In our outfit someone was hurt almost each day. A near drowning with an heroic and dramatic rescue was unextraordinary.

Perceptions

The war and our total active immersion in it, looking back on it, was so much more dangerous than I perceived it at age 19. I had adapted and, like my buddies, habituation to our fate made attitudes towards death and danger rather cavalier. Death's shadow darkened every man, but we were blind to it. Most of us were teenagers when sent to Vietnam. Such young men are oblivious to life's brittleness. We knew objectively that when a slug of metal rips through a vital organ or artery – you're dead. Emotionally, however, our tender minds could not stretch around the notion. We were immortal. Each of us thought death or serious wounds would happen to many of us, but he would somehow be spared. Almost no man squares with his own demise until his last breath. The enigma of war holds a profound mystery of life and death and I did not rush to the answer. None foresaw emotional and psychological implications which were conceived in combat, gestated in denial, and spawned years later in civilian life.

My emotional memory of the war is fresh and easily resurrected involuntarily by many things – certain music, for instance. Curiously, however, I retain no emotional memory of fear. I well remember a concern that death or worse would meet me there. I mentally calculated odds of survival grounded on weird meaningless formulas based on our losses. If death were to come to me there, I wished to be stricken early rather than after months of effort and misery. But I cannot resurrect fear in any form. Certainly fear and terror regularly coursed my organs, but memory rejects them now. Perhaps their visits were once too commonplace, or are suppressed beyond summon.

Rogers

Rogers was one of my best friends. He had been in Vietnam for some months when I arrived and was the first old timer to befriend me. I was assigned to his M-60 machine gun team. Richard Winegard was the gunner, Rogers served as the assistant gunner, and I was the ammo-bearer. Winegard had been there for a long time, traveling by ship to Vietnam with the First Cavalry Division when it deployed to Vietnam in 1965. He was a veteran of the Ia Drang campaign and kept a hunting knife on the strap of his GI butt pack. Thus when he lay prone, the butt pack, with knife atop, protruded one foot above the ground. The knife had 2 bullet strikes from Ia Drang and I had heard that he was the only surviving C Company machine gunner from that operation. Winegard was short, very quiet, and I liked him. He was sent back to the States within a few weeks after I arrived. I remember sleeping next to him on the ground by our gun position. The temperature was hot, but he was freezing and trembling uncontrollably. He had malaria and was evacuated never to return.

Rogers was now the gunner and he and I made a great team. A Boston Blue Blood from a wealthy family, he attended college before he volunteered for the paratroopers. During the summer of 1966 in Tuy Hoa, Rogers and I took the machine gun with a night ambush patrol led by an incompetent staff sergeant. He commanded only obedience, not respect, and established himself in the safest available location. He placed Rogers and me 20 yards in advance of the other men at the apex where two trails merged into one. The trails then proceeded towards our other positions. The site offered no cover or concealment. It had the benefit of only a small VC spider hole, or foxhole, nearby. I checked it for punji stakes. There were none. Punji stakes are bamboo sticks sharpened to a needle point, smeared with human feces and set firmly in the ground at an angle or in a foot trap. An ankle or calf wound from one caused a nasty infection. In some areas the punji stakes dotted the landscape, poised for a GI to stumble into or sit upon them. Usually they were rotten and broke off without puncturing the skin.

Rogers set the gun to cover the approach of both trails. The tactical layout of the ambush was poor and our gun position was suicidal. Rogers and I were furious, but compliant. He set the gun right on the trail, lay behind it and placed me in the spider hole to feed the ammo belt into the machine gun. He matter-of-factly instructed that if he were hit to roll him aside and continue to fire from the hole. Rogers had quality. That night was sleepless, but uneventful.

Rogers was evacuated to Japan with malaria, but returned to the field, though weakened. He eventually rotated home in one piece and I missed him. Rogers gave me an old patrol cap that Winegard had given to him and which had been camouflaged with

Richard Rogers and I posing with our machine gun. Note the safety-razor field haircut.

a magic marker. We exchanged letters few times after I returned home. He attended Officer Candidates School, and received a commission. We lost touch. I thought of him often over the years and determined to look him up someday, even though Richard Rogers was a very common name in the Boston area. The search began months before I was to visit Boston to run the Boston Marathon in April of 1993. Through a series of communications with Washington DC, I learned that he returned to Vietnam as an officer and was killed in action by mortar fire while again serving in the First Cavalry Division. More investigation led me to the local funeral director who buried Richard and had known his family. To my great disappointment, despite earnest attempts, including a feature in *The Boston Globe*, I was unable to locate any of his family members. Denise and I visited his grave in a remote corner at Island Pond Cemetery near West Harwich, Massachusetts. Was it possible that he had been dead as long as we had been married? And all those years I wondered what life had dealt him. How I wish Richard Rogers had lived. He had so much to offer. That old cap is framed on my den wall.

14

HEADS UP

Tree Burst

Our small patrol once survived unscathed from an artillery near miss. Actually, it was a direct hit. We took a mid-day chow break on a small bamboo-topped knoll overlooking lush terrain that sloped away before us. All were relaxed, helmets off, sitting in a tight circle near the base of the knob. While we ate, C Company's artillery FO (forward observer), Lt. Garaby; and Weiss, his RTO, via radio directions called in artillery fire ahead along our route of march. They walked the explosions at intervals along the trail. The knoll lay between the distant supporting howitzers and the impact zone. Precautionary, preemptive artillery support such as this was standard practice. We paid no attention as the harmless first spotter or smoke round sputtered in ahead trailing a white plume. After a short lull to adjust the fire, kerbooms from high explosive shells split the humid air as their detonations traveled, one after another, down a route in the vegetation on the low ground ahead, steady and sequenced not unlike a rubber ball descending a flight of stairs.

Then a millisecond after I heard a whooshing sizzle sound, like radio squelch, a thunderclap explosion shook the earth loose, and in slow motion, shreds of branches and leaves flung about in a staccatoed vibration as I flinched to the ground, and pretzeled up into my helmet in anticipation of the next incoming round. It passed overhead.

The blast was a dreaded tree burst. The 105 mm howitzer shell's arc from the distant gun to the other and lower side of the knoll intersected the top of the crowning bamboo clump. It detonated there and showered the area around us with hundreds of vicious shrapnel shards. Shredded bamboo lay everywhere. I was unhurt, but thought that certainly most others were wounded or worse. The world was mute for a moment then sounds grew stronger and stronger, obscured by a fading ring. Men hollered in panic. Driscoll walked by helmetless and dazed. A four-inch shard protruded from his smoking ammo pouch. It had detonated his rifle rounds in there. His jungle jacket was darkly splattered – not blood, but peach juice. The shard blew from his hand an opened can of C-ration peaches which he had been eating. He was a short timer and walked about dazed and numbly repeating "Why ain't I dead? Why ain't I dead?". Others experienced perforated clothing, gear, and even weapons, but amazingly no shards had pierced flesh or bone. We moved on. Another day in paradise. Ever after I flinch when an unexpected momentary sputter of hissing radio squelch meets my ears. The sound resembles incoming artillery or mortars the second before impact.

Smoke Round

The claim that an artillery spotter round is harmless does not hold if it decapitates you. These shells have no explosive charge, but are filled with a substance that emits a white smoky contrail for a few hundred yards prior to impact. Thus, if the target's map coordinates or reference point transmitted to the gun battery are inaccurate, our men are not blown up. The visibility of the smoke round allows easier radio adjustment of the subsequent high explosive shell's point of impact.

Most evenings as we prepared perimeter defensive positions, artillery fire was pre-plotted to strike nearby outside the foxholes so it need not be adjusted in haste if we were attacked. Smoke rounds popped about frequently outside the perimeter these evenings as the FO coordinated the fires for ready availability.

Once, however, as Dougher and I walked side by side within the perimeter a S-H-U-U-S-H radio-squelch-like momentary sound rocketed between us from above and behind, and thudded to the ground a few feet to our front. There was that quick, lethal sound again. Our startle sparked an automatic flinch – which, by nature was obviously too late. A 105 mm smoke round had split the distance between us, passing within two feet of our heads. Nearby gawkers flung the usual sardonic comments at us and validated our casual verge-of-death event. Had it been a high explosive round we would have been just two grease spots on the sand. Sometimes it was hard to keep your head.

Night Sniper

But I kept mine. I mean that literally. My helmet shed that crushed rock when the wild- fire raged towards us, and fate pressed that 75-pound smoke round to the side, just enough to spare my head. Fate would offer no quarter to Dougher's head in a few weeks, but she graced mine once more.

C Company trapped an enemy force in a small village, encircling it from surrounding muddy rice fields. The gridwork of paddy dikes offered natural breastworks. Rather than safely walking or crawling in the muck to check on my squad that night, I stayed dry by quietly walking along the top of a dike. It was elevated a few feet above the paddy. I assumed the darkness offered concealment. The dry route followed a dike wall directly toward and quite close to the village before angling perpendicularly on an intersecting dike to my furthest squad position which anchored the right flank of 3rd platoon.

The enemy was taking my measure. As I arrived at the joint of the right angle of the paddy dikes, which was the closest point to the village, I was evidently silhouetted in the darkness. A burst of automatic fire cracked by my ear; bright lasers of tracer rounds flashed by. At least one round was so near, it seemed as if I felt its warmth. After that it was the low crawl for me. As it turned out C Company was spread too thin. There was a wide gap on the flank and many NVA escaped to the right of where I was fired upon.

Bennie

Earlier that day we lay on our bellies there in the ripening rice under sporadic small arms fire from the village. Once in a while I raised up to look towards the source of the fire, but saw nothing. Bennie Holbrook reclined on his back a few yards to my side, his helmet a pillow, casually reading a paperback. I told him to be more alert and face the village. Bennie responded that he could see nothing to shoot at anyway, so he might as well relax a bit. It was true; I do not remember even firing my weapon that day. After a few hours nature called Bennie, but he dare not raise himself to squat because the firing had resumed and rounds zipped through the rice above our heads. Then nature shouted, and finally she must have screamed at him. He suddenly jerked up at the waist, shimmied his pants down a bit and horizontally then and there answered nature's summon. The vision appears ever after when I am mindful of Bennie. He was a good man, or rather teenager, whose amiable banter and humor are known only in memory. Bennie was a golden boy become gold star boy.

15

CHOPPER DOWN

Even if you live smart in Vietnam, Fate takes your right hand and Lady Luck grabs the left. The longer they hold on or the more times you challenge them, the more likely one or both will weary and let loose.

A number of slicks were enroute to C Company out in the bush to lift it to another anonymous LZ for a now long-forgotten purpose. We waited in a line of small groups parallel to where the slicks put down, their engines still whining. I picked up the machine gun and headed to the first slick. It was full so the door gunner waved me away. I just walked over to the second slick and piled in. We lifted off, the shaking engine clatter deafened all other sound. Looking over the front pilot seats, I could see the lead slick in the blue sky directly ahead. It floated gently up and down in relation to us, bobbing about the air. Then it slid below the plane of my vision. My view was limited, as I was seated on the floor with five or six others crowded with ammo, gear and weapons. The aluminum skin of those machines offered all the armored protection of a beer can.

The man on my left behind the co-pilot elbowed me pointing into the wind through the open side of the aircraft to the earth. The lead slick was way down near the ground, 500 feet below and dropping. Then it flipped on its side when the blades smacked the trees. It passed from sight as we flew on to an air assault. In a day or two we learned what happened to our guys. All had injuries, none serious under the standards of the time and place. My buddy, Fred Duncan, had been knocked out, badly cut on the lower forehead and bridge of his nose. He regained consciousness and got out before the machine ignited. The door gunner who had waved me off burned to death. Fred was disappointed he had not lost his eye so he could go home. All of us harbored such ideas and made similar imaginary hopeful trades.

16

ROCK FIGHT

Ft. Lonely

Even if Lady Luck jerks you safely out of peril, you may feel bad for getting the break. In November 1966 3rd platoon had been holed up at Ft. Lonely for a couple of weeks. We had settled in there longer than anywhere else before or after that. It was located in a large U-shaped valley near a coastal plain surrounded by highlands, the open end faced the South China Sea. C Company was charged with destruction of the Viet Cong infrastructure in the valley. We established night ambushes and raids and patrolled each day. Once during a night patrol, a B-40 rocket (also called a rocket propelled grenade, or RPG) fired at us struck almost dead on. The missile clattered harmlessly onto the rocky ground beside us – a dud. Accustomed to moving daily and digging a new foxhole each night, we were glad to establish a bit of permanence in this small one acre hamlet, surrounded by rice paddies and bordered by banana and palm trees. The platoon constructed defensive positions on the perimeter, the platoon CP (command post): Lt. Collins, SFC Juan Jose, Steinert, Duncan and Doc Nickels, nestled into a comfortable hooch in the center.

Our unit had been on active combat operations without any respite back at Camp Radcliff for many weeks. When we were last at that rear area base, our platoon received replacements, swelling it to 47 men. An old sergeant once said that the army rides a good horse to death. Third platoon was good horseflesh. After we left Ft. Lonely we numbered less than 20. Losses were from various causes: wounds, sickness, jungle rot, and rotation. We almost received more replacements while at Ft. Lonely. As a patrol from our platoon escorted these new replacements from the company CP near the coast to Ft. Lonely, they were ambushed and every man was wounded before reaching us. Thus, replacements equated to a net loss.

Enemy Sited

My assistant gunner, John Barra, from New Jersey, and a recent replacement named Talamantes and I, dug a strong shored up machine gun emplacement between banana trees with a good field of fire across the paddies. Barra talked often of the mafia and his family's Italian roots, especially his mother's luscious Italian meals. Talamantes loved to eat, too, and relished C-rations, especially when seasoned with acid spicy hot sauce and peppers that his family mailed to him. He claimed peppers were too mild if they failed to raise sweat on the back of his neck.

November 19, 1966 looked to be an easy day for my gun team, just guarding the perimeter, reading or writing letters. One squad was on a multi-day patrol and 3rd platoon also had an observation post on the hillsides bordering the valley to the north. I had just finished shaving in the brackish gray water drawn from the well fronting a thatched-roof hooch near our position. A man sent from the platoon CP said that an enemy squad with a crew-served weapon was heading in the direction of the foothills nearby. Our observation post there had spotted them moving in the valley. Lt. Collins told me to bring the machine gun to pin them down in a firefight before they reached a boulder-strewn cave complex. My adrenaline pumps jumpstarted. Barra, Talamantes and I quickly moved out, along with six others.

Our destination was less than one hour away. We double timed much of the way hoping to arrive before the enemy and set up a hasty ambush. They were waiting. We approached as the curtain rose on a gorgeous natural arena for the deadly drama unfolding. A series of waterfalls and rivulets bubbled, splashed and whirlpooled pristine water over and among a jumble of gray granite boulders piled up the hill mass like giant cannon balls pyramided in a park. Sunbeams danced seductively from eddy and flow, highlighting tiny quartz gems glistening in the rock. A fulsome beauty of tropical vegetation, lush and fecund from marriage of moisture and heat, surrounded and interspersed the tableau.

Our posse edged ever closer to the bandit stronghold. Then suddenly, wet Ho Chi Minh sandal tracks on hot sunstruck rocks – trod just minutes before – pointed the way. Approaching a chest-high boulder at a crouch, Lt. Collins and Sgt. Jose, side-by-side, slowly rose to peek over. A lone bullet snapped between their heads and over me. They flinched back down. I can still hear Sgt. Jose's loud eloquent standard all-purpose comment in his pleasant Hawaiian *bonhomie*: "shit, piss, hell, damn, fuuugh." We laughed like hell.

Cave Action

Here are the events of the following several hours which are spiked into my memory. We fanned out working among the boulders and rocks near what we would soon discover was the enemy lair. Jose and Collins spread us out so as to cover what was believed to be the main cave opening. There were several outlets. Explosions interrupted the gentle pattering of the waterfall as we heaved hand grenades into rocky enclaves. They sent me with the machine gun to cover a trail leading into our flank from the hillside. I quickly set it up on bipods a very short distance down the path on that approach and organized the ammo. The action perceived by each man was singular – compartmentalized and isolated among the boulders.

It became a siege. Barra and Talamantes remained to help the others cordon off the cave entrance area. Sporadic shooting and explosions continued. The rest of 3rd platoon was summoned for reinforcement. The long-range patrol, coincidentally located on the high ground above the battleground, worked down towards the upper limits of the enemy stronghold.

Apparently, many of us lay in open view of enemy sharpshooters hidden in strong firing ports, immune to our rifle fire and grenading. It seemed that each time a GI moved he drew fire. In a desperate effort to dislodge the enemy, CS (tear gas) grenades were thrown towards a likely source of their fire. The unbearable choking vapor spread in a wispy haze through the stony scene. We carried gas masks, but moisture often neutralized their filters. By this time I was back near what we thought was the cave main entrance. The gas spread to me and I donned my mask; it worked. Though barricaded in their rock stronghold, at least one NVA was very close. I could clearly hear him just a few feet away, wheezing with slow shallow breaths as if he used an apparatus to mitigate the tear gas. Those boys were hard-core tough!

Casualties

Then a rifle cracked nearby and Barra screamed in a panic then bellered incoherently something about cutting up his leg. My impression was that the NVA had Barra and had begun to butcher him. Talamantes shouted that he had reached Barra and Barra was shot through the thigh. Immediately another shot rang out there. While aiding Barra with a tourniquet, Talamantes had leaned into the NVA's restricted arc of fire from his small firing vent. The bullet crashed through Talamantes' jaw bone and nearly severed his tongue. I recall little about evacuation of these and other wounded except that Talamantes walked to the medevac chopper, which landed in a nearby rice paddy. I wondered how he could ever enjoy food again.

I looked into the vestibule of a cave and could see the gore from one enemy who had been killed by a grenade. An observation helicopter hovered low above to resupply us with grenades. I stood on a large exposed rock outcropping. A few feet above me the helicopter gunner/observer dropped a case of white phosphorus grenades to me, one grenade at a time. I then threw each of them to Sgt. Stewart, who stood on a lower rock closer to the entrance; he in turn pulled the pins and tossed each into the cave – a bucket brigade of fury! It was an utterly exhilarating event with the noise and blade blast from the helicopter, the concussion of the explosions and the expectation of being shot at the next moment.

Lt. Collins requested a flame thrower, a weapon wholly unfamiliar to us, to burn out the NVA. Higher authority responded that the nearest flame thrower was in Saigon and could not reach us for days. So much for the modern army. Then several jerry cans of aviation fuel arrived. GIs poured it into likely cave apertures and ignited it. There was no apparent result. By this time the remainder of C Company was en route to the scene. A four-man infantry flamethrower team from the Pacific War 22 years earlier could have killed these cave dwellers at cheaper human cost than we paid that day.

Men from other C Company platoons were shot, too. The mortar platoon leader, a short second lieutenant, charged uphill at an NVA firing hole while firing his rifle John Wayne style from the hip. The sniper shot once, striking the lieutenant in the knee. He hollered "ouch" and rolled down the hill. My friend from mortar platoon, Preston Polk, was wounded in the abdomen when a bullet struck the ammo pouch on his belt. It ignited his own ammo, driving bullets into him, exposing his entrails. He fell into the rocks and could only be extracted by helicopter cable lift. I watched as he was winched up to the helicopter. The enemy fired at him on the way up. He died.

That night a squad of GIs guarded the cave area and the rest of us returned to Ft. Lonely. By morning the enemy survivors were gone, having somehow escaped during the night. Their number remained unknown, but we suspected only a few caused so many American casualties that day.

Afterwards

Adjacent to my machine gun emplacement located in a corner of 3rd platoon's irregular perimeter was another three-man position. One other man and I returned to these two positions that night. All four of the others had been shot. Only I remained from my gun team. The odds came up one-in-three this time. I was just mid-point in my one-year tour. My prospects seemed poor. It was disheartening. Barra and Talamantes were both gone – their suffering unseen, their recovery unknown. They joined the growing band of ghost soldiers. They were men whom you really knew. You discussed all things on young men's minds. We talked of personal and intimate details of our lives and families. I knew their plans and dreams. In an instant they were gone forever – become ghosts. I was alone in the quiet darkness. The day's clamor and confusion vibrated on. A cloud of loss and sadness descended. It hovers about me to this day. It visits at the brightest of life's events. Then it floats in. It saddens otherwise delightful moments.

Later that night Marshall Storeby was sent to me from another squad. The awful events which he related to me that night appear elsewhere, a dreadful close to a horrible day.

PONY TEAM

In late January, 1967 I led a three-man long-range patrol called a "pony team" somewhere in the highland wilds of Binh Dinh province. Actually, it was a long distance observation post. The mission was to observe an NVA infiltration route. A Huey helicopter transported us to a remote mountain valley. Two empty choppers for dummy insertions followed it in trail. All three flew in fast at treetop level. The first –our chopper – set down, hovering a few feet above the ground. We leapt off, all done in a few seconds as the two dummy choppers continued their flight. After the insertion our chopper rose and took up the tail-end position in the line of choppers. Theoretically, this procedure concealed our drop from enemy eyes and ears, it appearing that the three choppers flew uninterrupted, one behind the other.

Jungled mountainsides cradled the valley checkered with patches of bamboo and cane, uncultivated rice terraces and elephant grass. At the mission briefing I was ordered to establish a position on the high ground. At dusk, half-way up the hill mass, we passed into and through a deserted NVA temporary base camp. There were signs and smells of recent occupation. Bamboo tables and mats, hammocks, discarded uniform scraps, cold cook fires and fighting bunkers came into view as we snaked through the trees beneath the jungle canopy. A pungent musty odor we recognized as the smell of enemy hung in the still air. It was eerie.

I eyed a suitable hideout and after dark we circled the wagons there. From concealment we observed the valley floor and across to the opposite massif in the daylight when it was not obscured by clouds. Each day in the dusk we re-located our den 100 meters away. Calling in artillery fire on a file of NVA binoculared across the valley was the only break in monotony.

After a few days the battalion commander's chopper circled high above. He admonished me for locating at elevation where it was impossible to monitor any valley trail activity after dark. I responded that we were positioned exactly where his operations officer had dictated. The colonel did not care; we moved immediately. Three young GI's were soon to learn about fishing from the bait's perspective.

New Site

The rest of our stint we spent in the valley on a narrow reed-covered sandspit nestled between a shallow creek and a four-foot-high bank. Atop the bank a trail enclosed by knee-high vegetation ran parallel to the creek, crossing it 25-30 yards upstream. Our view of the trail was mostly screened by bamboo growth except to our immediate front.

We hunkered in the rain and boredom, vainly trying to keep our lit cigarettes dry for more than two or three drags. Fortunately, our recently acquired GI sweaters softened the night chill. I was amazed that Bennie Holbrook was not only able to find sweaters in a tropical climate, but also steal them. He was a true scrounger.

Headquarters radioed that our mission was extended for three days and asked if we wanted food resupply. I refused. It was out of the question; helicopter delivery would likely have compromised our location. Our chow was gone, only a few packets of instant coffee and hot chocolate remained. A can of C-ration peaches lay secretly hoarded in my pack for a last minute morale builder. Bore upon by the menacing environs and elements – girdled in infinite time – benumbed by misery and gloom – we three complacently endured. We chatted in low tones and coughed unavoidably. Physical discomfort was no stranger, but hunger was new. It was piling up in my stomach.

Surprise

On January 25th a platoon or company-sized NVA force nearly jumped us. We sat idly between stream and bank in a close triangle. Hays leaned against the trail bank next to the radio, I sat facing him and Ski lounged to my right. A faint rhythmic swishing sound whispered from the trail as something disturbed the knee high grass arching in over both sides of the footpath. As my eyeballs rolled up, a khaki clad NVA soldier walked four to five feet in front of and above me on the trail. His feet tread within two feet of Hays' head. My M-16 was positioned the wrong way across my lap. Surely the NVA could hear my pounding pulse. My eyes tracked the intruder as my fingers tiptoed to my rifle. Neither of my men realized the NVA presence yet. "Nobody cough or move," I screamed silently inside myself. Fright augments perception and petrifies memory. If that face had flesh, I would recognize it on the street today. Then another North Vietnamese passed with an AK-47 "Airborne Killer" assault rifle at the ready. If either had glanced slightly to their right, I would not be writing this. We sat point blank from the hereafter. He was the last of a two-man point element. By now my buddies read my body language. Suddenly the alarm drained from me as we hastily readied our weapons. The void filled with the fatalism of a matador.

Options

Should I let them go? At the mission briefing the operations officer clearly told me to avoid any engagement. No need to tell me that twice. What would we do if one of us were hit out there, cut off, outnumbered and surrounded ten miles from our unit? But we may be able to bushwack the NVA in or near the creek. Wasn't action called for? If those two were followed by a larger force there may be a flanker walking the creek. He might spot us and we would be dead. These options sorted through in an instant. All I had ever learned or experienced focused like sunlight through a lens, intensified upon that moment. It was a fulcrum of self-knowledge – a continental divide in life's journey. Nothing else mattered and nothing else would ever matter like that. This was the test.

I was game. The most invigorating and intoxicating feeling electrified my nerves. Was I focused! Hays stayed put and faced the rear. Ski, armed with an M-79 grenade launcher loaded with a buckshot round, and I crawled along the sandspit closer to the bamboo-shrouded point upstream where we knew the trail crossed the creek and our field of fire would be clear.

Kill

We got a pass on our mistakes of complacency and momentary inattention. The NVA did not get one. We waited, tense-fingered with weapon safeties off, eyes zeroed 30 yards out on the green blanket of growth where trail met stream. The leaves parted and that face beneath a bush hat peeked out of the vegetation and looked up and down stream. Then the khakied figure quietly dipped a sandaled foot into the calf high water, his SKS rifle inexplicably slung barrel down from his shoulder. I expected him to reach the other side and then cover the crossing of his buddy before the second man even entered the water, the correct tactic. They were kids, too – dulled by their plight which condemned them with a senseless error. Before the lead man was halfway across, the second man stepped out of the bushes into the stream. What a break for us! Both of them were in the open and focused on the water.

It was murder. We fired. Ski's shotgun round was a dud. He blazed away with his .45 pistol. I emptied a 20-round magazine. Both NVA reached the other side. The lead man dropped. Then the second went down. He crawled into the brush. Ski fired grenades after him. I summoned pre-plotted artillery. Explosions rained around us. We checked the body. He was warm and limp – sprawled on the stream side. I grabbed his brand new Chinese-made rifle from the water. The shellfire lifted. Our trio flat out ran several hundred yards. We hid in the middle of a sugar cane patch like fugitives – wet, hungry – in trouble.

Hays (left) and I on long-range observation post. Shortly after this photo was taken, 2 NVA surprised us as they passed on trail behind Hays.

Extraction

The NVA searched for us that night. We heard them jabbering and glimpsed flashlight beams slicing for us in the dark. Headquarters told me not to communicate by voice on the radio, but respond by breaking radio squelch with one or more clicks of the handset. Squelch is a whishing-sizzle-sputter sound akin to AM radio static, but louder and more stark. Our PRC-25 radios could be set on squelch. Any incoming calls or handset squeezes by other radios tuned to the same frequency would break the squelch.

Silence is golden. Hays suffered from pneumonia. As each hacking fit began, Ski and I rammed his face into a poncho liner – one holding the blanket and the other forcing his head into it. We were waterlogged and punch drunk with hunger and desperation, but we found humor in the preposterousness of the moment. Next to the mighty moment after the two NVA trod past, I mostly recall the emotion of humor from this now poignant incident.

We were extracted the next day, having been out there for seven days, no food for the last three and wet all the while. We did not get a rest and did not expect to. Our rifle company was engaged in operations and we simply rejoined our platoon. Too late for a choppered-in hot breakfast, we dined on sumptuous remnants of nasty mess hall baked bread which we swabbed in congealed bacon grease pooled in thermite containers. Nobody took any particular note. Me either. But killing a man and taking his weapon that could have killed you makes you different. The rifle was eventually stolen by a rear area captain, but I still have the bayonet. The date and my initials are carved into the stock.

Reflection

Recounting this event inflates its significance and gravity beyond how it seemed at the time. Years later I came to see it as an elemental mark. I have thought of it daily but told it seldom and never completely. It is remarkable that the affair was unextraordinary in that maelstrom of history. The boldness of decision and action – rather than irresolution and passive waiting – brought self-respect. Deep self-examination exhumed more. Killing mattered, too. It was the game there. The field was level.

18

BANGKOK BRIGANDS

Though we squeezed through that ordeal alright, afterwards I felt insecure without a sidearm. What if we had been somehow captured? I once had a .45 pistol, as did all M-60 machine gunners. Even after I no longer carried the gun, I kept the .45, but eventually all unauthorized .45's were confiscated. At my request, Dad purchased and mailed me a small .25 Baretta pistol with ammo. Fred Duncan's dad sent him a .25 Colt, even smaller than mine. They were unauthorized, of course. What could the army do: shave our heads, dress us in green, feed us bad chow, force us to sleep on the ground in the rain seven days a week for low pay, and invite foreigners to kill us? I always carried the .25 concealed on my pants, not in my gear, in the unlikely chance of capture.

During an incident while on R & R in Bangkok, Thailand this pistol likely prevented a murder – mine. My buddy, who was our FO officer, and I hired a cab to see the sights in the old (and off-limits) section of the city. After passing through miles of bustling exotic Asian metropolis, our cabbie drove onto a narrow ancient street, which widened into a remote cul-de-sac in a bad neighborhood. He could only have done so by design. A band of young brigands closed in behind the cab. The cabby's demeanor and body language indicated he was in concert with them in an obvious plan to rob two GI's flushed with cash. The barrel of that cocked handgun violently jammed against his temple – steel to bone like a brand – not only precipitated his immediate defection, it enlisted him in our cause. To our glee he rapidly u-turned and accelerated through the scattering would-be felons. When we reached our hotel, Garaby slugged him through the open driver's window. I still owe him cab fare. We were angry. Pitted and holster-worn, the pistol came home in my pocket. Airport security was unknown in 1967. I gave it to my daughter, Amanda, when she graduated from the Air Force Academy in 2000.

19

CHRISTMAS

Monsoon

The Christmas blues would have turned purple in my case. It seemed as if I had been in Vietnam for most of my life, and I was only midway through my tour – *if* my luck held out for another six months. I had been in the field for months on end and had become one of those old timers, well used but not yet worn out.

My unit was operating in and area known as the Crow's Foot and it rained continually. Mud was our constant companion. We were creatures of the mud. It was everywhere and we lived in it. During one monsoon downpour we were served "hot" chow which had been flown out to us. As I splashed through the chow line my mashed potatoes dissolved and flowed off the soggy paper plate with the congealed gravy in a gray waterfall. When I got the steak, I was bumped and it plopped from the flaccid plate into the mud. I picked it up, wiped it on my muddy pants and chomped it like a dog. It was delicious.

Rivers flooded. One came up instantly after we forded it on a patrol. A helicopter had to ferry us back across in relays. Re-supply or medevac was difficult and undependable in the fog. The monsoon solved my thirst problem, but replaced it with other nagging miseries. I have mentioned the foot and skin rot. Cold and wet replaced hot and sweaty. It was often difficult to keep a dry cigarette, but something that really sticks in my mind is no dry toilet paper. After mail calls I was able to improvise.

The ground war was still young at the end of 1966 and there was a Christmas truce. The concept was ridiculous and the enemy would not honor it to his disadvantage anyway. U.S. offensive operations ceased for a few days, but I doubt if GIs would have held their fire if opportunity presented. T'was the season to be jolly. In a most counter-productive and ironic display of good intentions, the psychological warfare team cruised in helicopters above the mud broadcasting Christmas carols on December 25th. Our guys detested the gesture.

Celebration

Fortunately I was in Bangkok on R & R, so Christmas for me remained only blue, while I painted the place red. C Company's artillery forward observer, Lt. Garaby, and I roomed together in Bangkok. We casually signed up at the airport arrival briefing to be Christmas dinner guests with one of the several offering American families stationed there. Garaby and I bought civilian clothes, souvenirs and bronzeware to be sent to our families, ate a big steak and got drunk. The hotel radio played Christmas music, but we clicked it off and tried to tune out any suggestion of the holiday and its memories.

The next day we acted on the invitation at the home of an Air Force officer, his wife and cute four-year-old daughter. Another guest, a distinguished looking non-combatant Army colonel with sweater and pipe, drank brandy in the den with the host. The home was resplendent with symbols of all that Christmas meant to me. The kitchen table was lush with holiday snacks, cider and cookies, surrounded by the aroma of candles, turkey, ham and fresh bread. A festive dining room table setting sparkled and beckoned, displayed upon pristine linen in the lambent Christmas tree light. The child in fancy dress and patent leather shoes put me mindful of my childhood holiday innocence, excitement and wonder. She proudly informed us that there would be gifts for the guests after dinner, but Santa would not visit until late night. The scene was an exemplar of cleanliness, civility, generosity, beauty, warmth and home.

In contrast, Garaby and I were awkward, boorish and self-conscious. American civilians were aliens. My rank was only an E-4 and the presence of most officers made me uncomfortable. But Garaby was a buddy and felt as misplaced as I. We had just been out in the bush for over 100 continuous days. The dark world starkly revealed to me for those past months, and the animal-like existence until just three days before, conjured in me a sense of uncleanliness, unworthiness and confusion more intense even than I would feel later upon my return home.

Garaby and I cowered in the kitchen with the beer and snacks despite the hostess' gentle entreaties to join the men in the den. Our need to avoid the fluster of a homey Christmas that to us was not and could not be Christmas, outweighed our manners. I had not had Christmas for two years and knew its spirit and special feelings could not be faked. Without discussion Garaby and I had a meeting of the minds. At an opportune moment we bolted out the back door with not so much as a good bye or thank you and bee-lined for the beer and the band at the Navy Club downtown.

This incident comes to mind each Christmas. It brings regrets to this day. I lacked the words and the maturity to explain to those kind hosts why we felt compelled to leave abruptly without explanation or excuse. The reason was ineffable anyway. I just knew I had to leave. Our conduct appears rude in timing and in deed but one who understands knows that it was mitigated by a dash of respect and consideration for them. We did not want our uncouth and base presence to invade their beautiful Christmas celebration. We had been to the other side and were no longer worthy.

20

CHICKEN SHIT

The cause of one bitter army aftertaste was its frequent and plentiful servings of "chicken shit." The recipe is any meaningless, unnecessary, non-functional duty or requirement which is burdensome or imposing and almost always petty, making army life more miserable than it needs to be. The chef is a higher ranking person or anonymous authority – higher headquarters.

The nastiest dishes are served to the infantry. The menu is long and diverse. The development of Camp Radcliff from raw wild-west jungle to a military metropolis whetted the garrison army's fetish for personal appearance. Uniform regulations required name tag, rank, insignia and division patch to be sewed on a soldier's fatigue jacket. This was no problem for rear echelon people, including the MPs who enforced the edict. It gave some soldiers who actually fought the war a dose of chicken shit.

MPs

My assistant gunner, John Barra, went to base camp to leave for R & R. To get there from 3rd platoon's permanent wanderings out in "Indian Country" you helicoptered from the field to a division forward base, and there hopped a C-130 or Caribou transport plane to Camp Radcliff. You hitchhiked and walked a few miles from the airstrip to C Company billets.

Barra received a new fatigue jacket in the field to replace a torn or rotten one. Insignia was impossible to get out there. It had to be purchased from the Vietnamese in An Khe, the town adjacent to Camp Radcliff, because these items had been sold to them on the black market. Instead of a respite for a combat soldier where it could have been provided, Barra was busted by the MPs for his lack of uniform insignia. He suffered senseless delay and hassle which required the intervention of a battalion staff officer to resolve.

Fitness

    Quasi-civilization of base camp awakened the airborne tradition of a morning run and physical training for the rear echelon people of our battalion. That was fine for them, but when applied to the grunts in from field duty chicken shit happened. When fighting soldiers were back there, a well-deserved rest and long sleep was not possible. They were rolled out early for the morning fitness regimen. The injustice infuriated me. Wherever the army sent me and whatever it ordered me to do, I could always count on frequent snacks and occasional banquets of chicken shit.

Decapitation

    Bagley once shot a running VC with an M-79 grenade launcher. The 40mm grenade struck the nape of the man's neck and decapitated him. The VC had broken cover near the patrol so it was a short range shot. Bagley was himself wounded from the blast. A high ranking officer later flew over the area where the headless corpse lay sprawled in the open. Angered at what he thought was a mutilated corpse, the officer radioed the patrol leader and severely chastised him. After the facts of life about the effects of explosives on flesh and bone were explained, the complaining officer relented. Then he ordered another patrol to return to the area for the sole purpose of burying the body, apparently so others flying over the area would be spared the ghastly scene. Needless effort exerted, unnecessary risk assumed – for the sake of appearance. It was enhanced chicken shit.

Incidentally, I did not attend the patrol. Bagley had borrowed my Special Forces tiger-striped bush hat that my boyhood friend, Pete Bernstein, had given me when I saw him in Nha Trang. Bagley gave it to others in the patrol to return to me before he was medevaced. Sgt. Arthur was later wounded while wearing the hat, too. My lucky old hat molders in a frame in the den.

21

TANK ESCORT

Tanks had no business in the remote territory in which we usually operated. They were of little use against guerilla and main force VC units and the NVA, which were light infantry. Most terrain was passable only on foot. There were virtually no roads other than a few sub-standard highways. Even in the dry season, tank treads churned down through the paddy hardpan and floundered in the mud. But then the career tickets of some armor branch officers needed to be punched.

The infantry seemed always to be expendable. One would think that the purpose of tanks was to support the grunts, but from my vantage the role was reversed. Third platoon was the "escort" for several M-48 tanks for a couple of days. We packed on to the lumbering contraptions and jerked along with them, clinging like a baby orangutan to its mother. Since we were ordered to ride rather than walk near the tanks, I discerned no purpose for being there, and we felt like sitting ducks.

The machines got stuck frequently, often requiring the services of a tank retriever, the armored equivalent of a wrecker, to extract them. When one tank broached a hedgerow, the enemy set off a powerful command detonated mine, placed there, no doubt, for the sole purpose of destroying a tank. The explosion seriously damaged it but, luckily, injured none of the crew or infantry riders. Our platoon provided perimeter security for the tanks that night. One tank fired a "beehive" or shotgun-like round, consisting of hundreds of one inch steel darts, into the darkness at some real or imagined threat. The following day the tankers retrieved the damaged tank and we accompanied the armor to its destination without event, and then walked back to our starting point. The undertaking seemed senseless to me, but I was not a party to the big, or even the tiny, picture.

We "escorted" M-48 tanks for two days. A command detonated mine disabled one. SFC Juan Jose and I joked as we posed, but we felt like sitting ducks.

22

BREAKING POINT

Men of an infantry platoon experience the same activity at certain moments, such as an air assault or troop movement, but the specifics of perception and view were as varied as the number of men involved. Every man had a different war and his background and makeup accounted for his unique adaptation to it. The common stimuli that bore upon combatants would today be called stress. Among its ingredients: violence, fear, filth, physical discomfort, boredom, exhaustion, sleeplessness, homesickness, and uncertainty. The direct cause was the VC and the NVA and accordingly, they were the immediate object of our hatred and anger.

We loved to hate a sinister and often unseen enemy who struck by booby trap, ambush and sniping. Such tactics were frustrating to a force such as ours with overwhelming mobility and firepower. That was the big picture. Down on the face-to-face, ass-in-the-grass, here-and-now the enemy had the killing power we did, everything of instant and usual importance, except artillery support. And generally he chose when and where to use it. An air strike, for instance, may not be useful if the enemy is too close or the aircraft one or two hours away. My war was not like that anyway. It consisted mostly of up close and personal individual, squad, or platoon-sized encounters more reminiscent of the gunfight at the OK Corral rather than Omaha Beach.

We secured no ground, liberated no occupied towns, assaulted no beaches. Not that the cutting edge of the tool needs to check the blueprint, but we grunts were not privy to our unit's goal – immediate or long term. Tomorrow was always unknown. We seemed to always aggressively search out and kill the enemy. But you cannot kill what you cannot see. Days passed without laying

Third platoon occupied LZ Charles, a forward observation post outside Camp Radcliff, after it had been overrun by the enemy. A shot-up bunker is seen in the rear.

an eye on him. Dismal weeks of immense effort plodded. Hardship and suffering were bestowed in the quest. There were heavy blocks of time. There were losses from the elements and booby traps. There were months of no real relaxation. There was danger – patient, in wait. There was Death – latent and coiled.

The effect of these stressors was gradual and cumulative. They etched everyone. In time their corrosiveness dissolved the mantle of civilization in some. The pressure cracked many men, some temporarily; some crushed. The process was not dramatic or abrupt. It was unnoticeable in the atmosphere of lunacy in which infantry war happens. The corrosion is subtle – sinister and unseen – crumbling restraint and taboo from the inside out, until the pipes burst.

Gervase

This brings the narrative to a man named Gervase. His rank was E-4 when I arrived in 3rd platoon. He was just another faceless member of the rank and file. He prided to formerly have been stationed with an airborne company in Alaska and displayed "Artic

Paratrooper" on his helmet camouflage cover. Butch Paszkiewitz had also been in that company and he and Gervase were buddies there. Butch was an excellent combat soldier. I respect his boldness and solid dependability.

After a few months Gervase became weapons squad leader, although he had not yet been promoted to sergeant, the rank warranted by a squad leader. But he had the authority and it transformed him overnight. He became a tyrant who relished to wield his new stature in many meaningless menial ways that were contrary to good leadership. For example, he required us to shave every day whether or not we even had drinking water. He once required a man to dig and refill a "six-by-six", a six foot square hole into the ground, for a minor infraction. It was an obviously unwarranted punishment. This was chicken shit. It rolls down-hill from above in a combat zone by the ton anyway and your immediate boss should not raise the heap.

Otherwise he was a fearless and competent soldier, though rash. For no reason he disarmed Chinese potato masher grenades by tinkering in through the bottom after removing the wooden handle. American fragmentation grenades had a 4 or 5 second fuse. Before throwing one Gervase "cooked it down" to within 1 or 2 seconds of detonation. I was more nervous about his grenade-throwing than his intended targets. Such show off and reckless behavior made me uneasy.

The tyrant turned mean and hard. Gervase began senseless cruelty, casually stabbing cats and exhibiting unnecessary meanness to enemy prisoners. Some noticed his derangement, but it drew no comment. Then on a night patrol his friend, Paszkiewitz, was seriously wounded along with others. After that Gervase's complete moral deterioration became evident to me. Mistreatment of prisoners degenerated to cold blooded murder when he was ordered to escort two prisoners to the company CP. As soon as he was out of sight we heard firing and suspected what had happened. Gervase calmly claimed with a wink and a nod that they tried to escape and he gunned them down.

Near in time to these incidents he led a small half-day patrol into the high ground west of Ft. Lonely. Gervase was point man and I was next behind him carrying the radio. We entered a football-field-sized open plateau broken by a cluster of large imposing boulders and bordered by cactus and wait-a-minute bushes and their stiff narrow needle-pointed leaves. Walking in single file, we jumped two enemy soldiers armed only with grenades. They were crouched near the rocks monitoring a transistor radio connected to several used GI radio batteries, and tuned to our company frequency. Were they enemy intelligence officers? Luckily, they did not see our approach over the open area where a sudden grenading would have been lethal. It was mutual surprise, but we were standing and had rifles. Gervase, being on point, shot and wounded one. The second leaped so swiftly into the rocks and cactus that he ran out of his Ho Chi Minh sandals and escaped down the hillside. I have never seen a man move so quickly. As naturally and thoughtlessly as smashing a bug, Gervase pointed the muzzle of his M-16 near the wounded enemy's head and pulled the trigger.

Not more than an hour later into the patrol a VC rounded a corner in the trail in front of us and came face to face with Gervase who instantly shot him. As he lay bleeding beside the trail, Gervase, his dark eyes as cold as a snake's, placed the barrel of his rifle in the man's ear and fired. This happened in less time than it takes to read about it. Brutality feeds upon itself and his sadism and bloodthirstiness grew. He had been struck by the sorcerer's wand.

Gervase's deterioration culminated in the rape and murder of a teenage Vietnamese girl for which he was sentenced to 10 years in Leavenworth prison. The horrid incident is related poorly and incompletely in Daniel Lang's book, *Casualties of War*, and is the subject of an even worse movie by that name. I have much to tell about the matter, but will not lengthen this narrative with it. They say that truth is the first casualty of war. Let us hope truth is not also the war's final death. The prognosis is poor. Lang failed to enlighten the reader as to the inhuman conditions, the prolonged exposure to danger and violence which propelled Gervase to moral collapse and methodic barbarity. His veneer of civilization peeled away and with it the distinction between legitimate violence and atrocity.

Others among us lost who they were in Vietnam, but none so completely as Gervase. He put a bullet in his brain in the early 1990s. The 3rd platoon hated what he did to that girl. War never excuses barbarity nor relaxes individual responsibility.

DOG

Some found who they were there. My very good friend Thomas E. "Dog" Dougher from Albany, New York did before he was shot in the head and killed. I was absent at the time. I hate that he is dead and that I was not there. Forever I will wonder if, and hope that, these facts are unrelated. Others told me that he was not wearing his steel pot, only the helmet liner and cloth camouflage cover. Such a stupid stunt was in his character. If I had been there he may have worn it. Dog was unconventional. Maybe it was because he was an orphan and a true fatalist.

When I arrived in-country, Dog was a hapless private. His reputation was that of a dud, a screw-up. The platoon sergeant, SFC Alonzo, a fierce and feared tyrant, hated Dougher and showed it at every opportunity. Dog was not promoted and Alonzo assigned any dirty hateful jobs to Dog. When I first met my platoon it was returning to base for a few days' rest after Operation Crazy Horse. No rest for Dougher. Alonzo detailed him to KP each day until we moved out again. KP was filthy, sweaty, hard work, mostly outside in the tropical sun lasting from pre-dawn to late at night. Dog – like Pvt. Prewitt in *From Here to Eternity* – took anything and everything that Alonzo, Vietnam and the world dished out. And he endured with a good-natured fatalism. For example, being at the mercy of the elements, we were usually either wet, and maybe cold and miserable; or thirsty and hot and miserable. Attitude is the key to coping. Dog had a unique one. If, for example, dry weather and a chance to dry out appeared, and our path encountered a puddle or wet ground, rather than walking around it like everyone else – Dog plopped in. He just laid down in the wet and mire without ever removing his gear. Why? Attitude. His theory: the rest of us would worry and fret about staying dry and then whine like hell when we could not; he spared himself the effort. He got wet and miserable straightaway. Afterwards comfort was no further concern. His motto: when the first drop runs down the crack of your ass you are soaked anyway. Whenever dry shod, our nature was to sidestep and tiptoe around mud holes and puddles in consideration for our stinking, jungle rotted feet. It never helped. Your feet always eventually got soaked. Dougher spared himself the trouble and splashed into the first pool he met.

After Sgt. Alonzo left, Dougher seemed to flourish. By then he was one of the more experienced troops, handy at many things, such as repairing weapons and gear. Our platoon had a futuristic night vision device called a starlight scope. It was bulky, very expensive and complex. Grunts were admonished to keep it dry. Ours was immersed during a stream crossing. It would have to be sent to the rear area for repair and somebody would be in for an ass chewing. Dog amazed us when – without any training and no instruction manual – he dismantled, cleaned and dried it, then reassembled the scope in perfect working order. No one else could even get it apart. He had innate abilities to deal with such things.

Enemy Saved

Dog did one of the bravest and craziest deeds ever. Our outfit was clearing an area previously held by an NVA battalion that had been destroyed mostly by artillery and air strikes. Slain enemy and body parts lay about corrupting and putrid in the tropical sun. The stench was indescribable. We were checking bunkers for weapons and stragglers. Dog volunteered to go in one so we grabbed his ankles and lowered him into the entry hole headfirst, flashlight in one hand and a .45 pistol in the other. Immediately he hollered to get out because he spotted two NVA in there with a rifle. Dog fired the .45 as one NVA reached for the weapon, shooting him through the breast from side to side beneath the nipple. We jerked Dog out and prepared to grenade the hole, a simple and safe resolution. Dougher begged us not to do it and insisted upon going in again to take the NVA out alive. When we lowered him back in I just knew they would kill him. How could they miss? But they did not shoot and somehow he got them both out without further violence. I wonder if that NVA ever knew that the man who shot him is also the man who saved his life.

Extension

Dog got a dog. Dougher saved a small puppy from a burning hooch and revived it by mouth-to-snout resuscitation. He mothered it and carried the pooch in a pouch on the side of his NVA rucksack. The pup's cute little head peeked over the canvas, bobbing to and fro with the tempo of his master's gait.

Dougher sensed his new-found value and he prided in his contribution to the group. Being an orphan may have factored in, too. Third platoon became his family. When his one-year tour ended, he volunteered to extend it for six months. This option was available to all, but few opted for it. To extend, as Samuel Johnson said about second marriages, represented the triumph of hope over experience. I knew six men who extended. Luck never lasts. All six were either killed or badly wounded. Shortly before our rotation date back to the states, Lt. Collins (then company executive officer) talked to Fred Duncan and I about extending for further duty in Vietnam. Fred was Lt. Collins' former radio operator and we were two of the oldest hands in the platoon. Lt. Collins knew us well. He was required to give us the pep talk about extending in Vietnam. He guaranteed our promotion to staff sergeant if we would extend our tour of duty. Off the record, however, he said that we should go home. After Dog extended, he took a one-month leave to the States. He met a girl and married.

Premonition

Shortly after he returned to Vietnam, Dog accidentally shot himself in the foot. He had a .45 pistol holstered with a round in the chamber and the hammer resting on the firing pin rather than safely held on half-cock. As he hoisted the radio on his back, its supporting brace slammed down on the hammer, firing the round between two of his toes. The bullet only peeled toe meat, not bone. It was impossible to avoid infection and heal in the filth of the field so he was evacuated to the division rear area at Camp Radcliff. By then we were very close friends. He was still in the rear area when I choppered there prior to an R & R in Taipei, Taiwan. Dog was broke so I gave him money. We went drinking that night at a nearby dingy beer shack.

He lay awake on his cot when I woke before dawn to hop a flight out. I bid him good bye, I would see him in four or five days. He replied "no you won't." I repeated that I would be back through the area soon before I returned to the field after my R & R. Dog said soberly that the doctor had declared him fit to return to field duty so I would not see him again. Then I said that if he were back with the platoon, I would see him when I returned to the field in about one week. Dog just replied that he would not see me again. At that time his comment did not register.

Taipei

I went on R & R to Taipei, Taiwan in late April 1967, and enjoyed none of it. My morale was particularly low. I got so drunk that I lost a whole day. I sobered up thinking it was, say, Wednesday, but it was really Thursday and I had no memory of the intervening day. The knees of my new civilian pants were torn and I needed a shave and shower. Luckily, I still had most of my money. There was still over one eternal month left in my Vietnam tour. A foreboding menace was staring me down.

One month of time passed in middle-aged comfort is but an instant. In Vietnam it is an era. I spanned a generation there in one year. The coming month, I sensed, was to be the rest of my lifetime. It was not so much that Fate would open death's cold door, it was that time – frozen and ice-jammed – would never thaw and flow once more to float me away into the future. I just could not envision the end.

By now home and homefolks were light years distant from the kaleidoscope of experience I had since my 19th birthday. All of my life had happened in Vietnam. Childhood and adolescence were a chimera – remote and phantasmal. Later attempts to retrieve my past self were useless. When I grabbed to embrace the world I left in 1966, it whipped aside like a web in the breeze. It was a gossamer filament, suspended within reach, only to spire away in the wake of my clutches. But that happened later in the States after *who I once was* settled back into my vision, but outside of my reach. For now any other existence – the past and the future – hovered in the clouds above my view. I was under a rock, in the darkness.

I was s*omebody* here. There was responsibility here. There was purpose here. People depended on me here. My place was here. All that I had ever done I had done here. Wasn't it all I could ever do? But so many had gone now; and I had seen so many come and go, yet there was a sort of distance from the newer guys; I never got really close to them. Even the three buddies I came to C Company with as a replacement over ten months ago were gone now. Montforti took grenade frags in his arm after less than two months. Lady Luck held Christina's hand for a long ten months, then she released him into a booby trap. It claimed a part of his leg. The fate of the third escapes memory. I drew breath from friendships – solid and strong as blue steel – forged here: Duncan, Jose, Hartnell, and Dougher. All of us except Dougher was due to leave soon. He had months yet on his tour extension.

Home connections were a force driven by mail and memory. But power weakens and drains over time and distance. How long before it is spent? Would I be able to merge into normalcy again? What was normalcy, now that I had gazed upon the bleaker aspects of existence? Would people accept me now? Would I accept them? Such unarticulated icy crystals of doubt coalesced and penetrated my resolve. They chilled confidence. They numbed hope. I lost sight of the end – snow blind in a deepening blizzard of dismay and despair.

Cam Ranh Bay, a major U.S. base on the South China Sea coast, held a transient barracks for incoming and outgoing R & R personnel. Upon returning to Vietnam from the joyless R & R at Taipei, I was sitting on my rack as Campbell, a man from our platoon, suddenly approached. He was en route to R & R. I was surprised to see a familiar face there. He said, "I'm sorry Sgt. Saunders, your good buddy, Dougher, was killed yesterday." I was pole-axed.

Breakdown

When I was a kid, adults would say that someone had a nervous breakdown. I did not know what that meant. Then Campbell's news crushed me. Now I have the meaning. I went totally haywire. That day and the next are a blur. I did not leave the bunk. Despondency – futility – hopelessness paralyzed me. All vestige of optimism and confidence was buried. The world was truly forlorn. It was shock, too. And self-pity. Was that silent sinister voice which beckoned Dougher clearing its throat for me? I scratched a severe letter to my father. I do not remember its content. Later I wished I had not mailed it. He did not deserve to know the truth.

The barracks emptied; the GIs were either going back to their units or leaving for R & R. I stayed put, alone and AWOL. I did not care about anything. That is all I remember; it was a very bad time for me. If I had been with Dougher that day he was killed, it may have ended differently. I have been told several times exactly how they shot him, but my mind's immune system seems to reject the information like disease organisms. My heart will not retain the details. The squad had made enemy contact and were tracking a wounded NVA. Dog was investigating an area by himself when he was shot in the head. His death made me feel so sick and empty, and I have cried about it so much and am very angry with myself when I do, because I always promise not to do it again. Dougher could have chosen a soft rear-area job as consideration for extending his tour for six months, but he wanted to stay with us. He saw death's approach. He warned me, but I did not hear. His courage extended far beyond duty. I call him to mind each day.

That illustrates something about male bonding under shared hardship and danger. To say we were like brothers is trite and inexact. Some of us were much closer. Some of us detested one another. There was no posturing, no pretensions, no phony manners; civilian social position or background mattered not. The war stripped each man to his essence. Extreme adversity limelighted one's qualities, good and bad. It broke down many. Young men do not fight out of patriotism, duty or other high-toned ideas. You may enlist or report for induction mindful of such concepts, but when war actually bites, you drive on because you have no choice, and seek the esteem of your peers. You would loath their disrespect worse than death.

Bennie Holbrook (KIA), SFC Juan Jose, Thomas Dougher (KIA), Fred Duncan, Schmidt awaiting spring 1967 airlift to unknown destination.

24

SCARED

Neither bravery nor cowardice is a permanent state. Sometimes you are brave and sometimes you are chicken. Usually you pendulate in between. I often heard it said that a GI is "scared" or he "got scared," or reference made to a time when he "was scared." It was not derogatory, rather just a description that at a certain time, the GI took counsel of his fear. So long as it affected no one else, it did not matter. The scared factor may come and go. It did not equate to cowardice. Every man was scared sometimes. It stayed with some longer or manifested itself to the extent that it was elevated to a status recognizable by others, but usually a temporary one. The malady more likely took hold or increased in frequency and intensity the closer one got to his rotation date. I was scared for two days after Dougher got it. Then I found composure and went back. Nobody knew.

Now on to Sgt. Anderson. He was the RTO for either the company commander or the first sergeant, an indication of a reliable and dependable soldier. He was promoted to Sgt. E-5 about the same time as me. Anderson and I were good buddies rather than close friends. Being in the headquarters element he was not out with our platoon much of the time, but we got on well together. He looked very young and had an easy and pleasant way about him. Like I said, he was a very good man, but he got scared. After he returned from an R & R, he stayed AWOL in-country. That is, he just did not go back to the war, but hung out somewhere in the rear area, a fugitive with no duty and potentially in big trouble. As if there could be bigger trouble than risking combat duty.

While Anderson was AWOL, "Top," the first sergeant, actually knew where he was. I had to go there en route to Camp

Radcliff to attend a short squad leaders' instructional course. Top asked me to find Sgt. Anderson and try and convince him to return to the company. There would be no sanction and he could keep his stripes. If he failed to return, Top would have to report him and consequences would follow.

That is what scared was. Though it would not be tolerated in a man who had not previously proved himself, Top understood that Anderson just had enough for awhile. It did not mean he was not a good man; did not mean he had not been a good man, and it did not mean that he would not be a good troop in the future. For now he was just scared and needed to pull himself together. Anyway, when I found Anderson, we had a long talk. He was broke and I lent him some money and helped him convince himself to return to duty. The first sergeant kept his word. Anderson kept his RTO job and his stripes. I wish I had left him scared and AWOL. He was hit by our own ARA (Aerial Rocket Artillery) and bled to death – all over his stripes.

25

THE DEAD

Death was different in Vietnam than it is here. It is not mysterious there, not candied like here with chemicals, cosmetics and organ music. It rides on your shoulder. You see the immediate and natural effect upon the human body. In war you become desensitized to it. Dead enemy soldiers were common. When we remained in one location for more than a few days, observing the same dead day after day, you learned to gauge how long since the living had been taken from a corpse by its skin color and extent of decomposition.

Theirs

Corpses do not age well in the tropics. They are quickly fly-blown and bloated, emitting an overpowering stench. Enemy bodies were denied human respect. They were objects of disgust – quickly looted for documents and souvenirs. Chivalry was unknown.

Our platoon relieved a unit which secured a small outpost outside of Camp Radcliff called LZ Charles. The enemy had attacked and overrun it recently and left several dead outside the concertina wire. The lips of one corpse had puffed out from bloat, baring the teeth. I was humiliated to see two men casually dismantle the teeth and jaw with pliers – a final gesture of hatred. It shamed us. Circumstance peeled away civilization layer by layer like an onion. For some the core unraveled.

A beautiful coastal plain near the South China Sea close to Bong Son dotted with hamlets and palm trees became the scene of slaughter. A substantial force of NVA was trapped and destroyed there largely by artillery and air strikes. Scores of them lay black and deliquescent in the hot sun. One appeared to be breathing. It was the wave-like gentle undulations of a chest full of teeming maggots. Another body farted putrescent gas as I passed by. C Company set up a perimeter a half mile away and sent in patrols and night ambushes to gather up weapons, munitions and NVA stragglers. Breezes carried the corruption to our noses, even at that distance. We could not eat much and when we did swarms of flies visited our faces. The stench clung to our clothing and gear like a cocklebur after leaving that abattoir.

After about ten days, higher headquarters ordered us to bury the dead. I was angered. So often the authors of such belated and ridiculous orders had little idea of the reality on the scene. Chicken shit happened again. By then burial was not possible; the bodies were too jellied to remain intact. We scooped some sand over a few.

Ours

Fortunately, the disparity in casualties between us and the NVA was so great, a dead GI was a rare sight. But it was a sobering one. The morning after a firefight in which C Company suffered 7 killed and 17 wounded, our dead – SSgt. Thompson, Sgt. Houston, Sgt. Travis Gary Walden, PFC Alonzo and the others – lay side by side on their backs. Their arms were risen – curled and stiff – as if beseeching heaven to send them home at last. Sgt. Houston and I had returned to the field together on a supply slick from LZ Hammond less than 48 hours before. The blast of the blades as the choppers lowered in blew away makeshift head shrouds on the dead like chaff. It filled their stony eyes with pallid sand – giving each a ghoulish eyeless death mask. Everyone hesitated and then Fred Duncan and I broke our trance and carried

Houston, then Thompson, to the chopper – one in a poncho and the other in a hammock. Fred does not remember it. I do not clearly remember the events leading up to the tragedy. But I recall that Walden very soon would have gone home alive. He and our friend and 3rd platoon buddy, Gerald Brown, had been close buddies through jump school and training. Brown stayed with Walden at Walden's home when they had leave before shipping to Vietnam. Brown promised Walden's mother that he would take care of her son. Walden's death hurt Brown.

Many friends became ghosts without dying. Wounded or very sick, they were instantly gone, often never to be seen or heard from again. Here one moment and vanished the next. No time or energy to grieve or even grasp the loss. Eventually you miss them always.

So I can shuck delicacy and concern for the reader here to describe in horrid detail what young death looks like in real life, not the kind we see on film or in funeral homes. But now, living a good life of ease and relaxation, I cannot resurrect what it used to feel like. I cannot feel some of those things now because I would not allow myself to do so at the time. Yet it has been an effort to keep quiet about them.

26

ATTITUDES

Fears

No one from our unit was captured by the enemy, few infantrymen were. Capture by the VC or NVA would doubtless have brought instant execution or agonizing death through disease and, perhaps, torture. Low rank infantrymen captured in South Vietnam would have been of little or no value to the enemy; certain death was inevitable. The NVA executed our wounded when they overran First Cav positions during the Ia Drang battles. I personally observed the effect of cruelties perpetrated upon helpless civilians who refused VC demands. During one of my first patrols, while close on the trail of some VC, we entered a Montagnard settlement. Montagnards were an indigenous tribal people of ethnic origin different from the Vietnamese. I was shocked to see a woman who had apparently displeased the VC visitors, for they had gouged out both of her eyes. It was pitiful.

To one reared during the Cold War years of the 1950's and 1960's, the Asian Communist world was remote and alien, as bleak and foreboding as the dark side of the moon. We knew of the maltreatment and "brainwashing" of American POWs by the Red Chinese and North Koreans during the Korean War.

Our situation, I thought, involved very little risk of capture, until an incident when two others and I were surprised by the enemy and I realized that capture was possible if we had been wounded, or stunned by grenades. Before that incident all .45 pistols, except those that soldiers were authorized to have, were confiscated and relinquished to the company supply sergeant, mine included. Thus, I had no side arm as back-up in the event my M-

16 rifle malfunctioned. Our old style M-16's were noted for jamming. But with the .25 cal. automatic pocket pistol hidden on my body I would never endure the humiliation and ignominy of capture. Capture was a fate worse than death in my eyes. We expected no quarter from the enemy anyway.

Hatred

I respect and admire men like Senator John McCain who, having suffered from the inhumane treatment and savagery of the North Vietnamese, after the war achieved a measure of personal accommodation with his past and, without bitterness or hatred, let by-gones be by-gones. Then he worked for rapprochement with the Vietnamese government. His example is a laudable model for peace and forgiveness. Like most fighting men, however, I cannot be brothers with once mortal enemies. The status *enemy* seems immutable on a personal level. I hold an involuntary grudge. To do otherwise would betray the bond with those comrades dead and alive, magnificent men, who shared war experiences and who stood by each other when it counted.

Although for me the fighting ceased many years ago, my hatred of the NVA did not abate, even with the end of our country's involvement in 1975. The war never ended in my mind. I remain shamed by the discordant feeling, but cannot deny it. Often I obsessed about killing NVA and repeatedly dreamed of choking one with my bare hands. This is weird. Even as late as 1997 I would dream about having a machine gun fight with a North Vietnamese soldier one-on-one, winner take all. There is no rational explanation for these involuntary illusions and they are aberrant to my adult family and professional life. Recognition and self acknowledgment of this character flaw failed to eliminate or weaken it. I stuffed it all, unexpressed, in my interior safe. But it had a time lock.

Aggressive offensive military operations during my time in the Vietnam War, the all-consuming physical and emotional effort, the loss of and suffering of my friends, and my sudden departure unscathed from it, allowed no personal finality to the experience. The business remained forever unfinished. Years later it was no more resolved than when I first returned home. The hatred had branded on my core. Hate is a bilious, unhealthy quality. It lays acid-like within and is personally limiting. However, around the year 2000 I sensed that my hate had dissipated. It seemed like much of the passion I always held for the enemy had seeped away, replaced by a sterile ambivalence. I do not know what precipitated the transformation, nor exactly when it occurred. Although I am heartened that it left, for some strange reason a void remains in its place. Perhaps its absence is the reason that I take pen in hand. One's greatest enemy is himself.

A SOLDIER'S HEART

Max

It is uneasy to view the enemy as human. We regarded them as "gooks," equal to vermin. A few instances, however, reminded me that they were human and, perhaps, revitalized my humanity. Combat rapidly erodes one's thin veneer of civilization. As a grunt infantryman I felt like the lowest creature walking the earth. Living like an animal and being treated like one, substantially lowered one's self worth. You become hard and wise in an animal-like style of self preservation.

Taking enemy prisoners was very common. You did not care what ultimately became of them, but assumed that VC and NVA prisoners were remanded to the custody of the South Vietnamese military or civil authorities where many would be brutalized and killed. Surely, that seldom happened, but then I thought it did. Oddly, I did not question any of this at the time, like so many things. It takes a lifetime to process what happened.

Our platoon once had an NVA prisoner with us a few days before it was possible to evacuate him. When re-supply choppers finally came in we kept him anyway. In the meantime, he had packed extra gear for us, dug foxholes, cooked chow and did odd-jobs like a handyman or servant. He was friendly. We liked him and called him "Max." He spoke no English, of course, but somehow we communicated. Human interaction changed a faceless enemy into a friend. Max was helpful in dealing with civilians. A group of women and children that we had moved out of their hamlet were inside our small nighttime defensive perimeter. In the night automatic fire ripped through the perimeter and the civilians became very agitated. Charged with their care, Max succeeded in calming them and keeping them down, preventing their panic and exposure to the fire.

Max seemed to enjoy staying with us; we treated him well. With as much food as he wanted and plenty of cigarettes, his lot was much better during his short time with 3rd platoon than with his own army. Then before an air assault the word came down that Max had to go. Rather than committing him to the tender mercies of the South Vietnamese as a POW, we gave him a rucksack filled with C rations, cigarettes and a poncho and gestured for him to leave. Like a shunned puppy he hung back. He looked so sad and frightened; we did not want him to go either. A lone NVA with a rucksack wandering that open valley would need luck to survive ambush and attack by American patrols and the ever-present searching of helicopter killer teams. I hope he survived the next eight years of war, but that is very unlikely. If so, do you suppose anyone would believe his war story of living in harmony with a U.S. airborne infantry platoon who re-supplied and then released him in a combat zone? Life is absurd.

Despite the cruelty of a few, Americans were kind and generous to civilians and children. Kids got all of our canned milk, and much candy and cigarettes. Vietnamese condoned children smoking. It was strange and amusing to see small children shamelessly and happily puffing away. We all smoked – weren't we kids too?

NVA Wounded

Mercy toward enemy soldiers often took the form of dispatching those who appeared too badly wounded to be saved and not worth endangering a helicopter medevac. I never did so myself, not out of altruism, but because I sensed I would regret it later. Others were always willing and some of these men have had much trouble and bad luck in civilian life. It was as SFC Jose, a Korean War combat veteran, always warned: misfortune visited those who were needlessly cruel to the enemy or committed atrocities.

One wounded NVA was so pitiful, that I must relate the memory. On a hillside near where 3rd platoon was positioned for several weeks at a small hamlet we called Ft. Lonely, our patrol stumbled across a critically wounded NVA hidden in the rocky foothills, overgrown in wait-a-minute bushes. He lay paralyzed on his back, a large shard of shrapnel protruded from his head and metal peppered his body. He had evidently been there several days, for the stench of gangrene insulted the air. Unbelievably, he was still conscious, but could move only his eyes. They rolled from side to side – wide, white and frenzied – while a dozen GIs gawked. There appeared to be no hope for him. A few men, especially a mean-hearted Cajun, wanted to end his misery on the spot, a not uncommon practice. But ironically the extent of his horrible wounds and the hopelessness of his plight transformed this enemy soldier from an object of hate to a receptacle of pity and sympathy. It was decided to medevac him. I doubt if he survived, but I take heart from the effort. His young visage remains in my mind's eye, face etched with fright and the furor of the fighting, and the gloom in his gaze reflecting the tragedy of that time and place.

The capture of a wounded NVA straggler hiding in a hamlet also incited my compassion. A bullet had grazed his lower abdomen from side to side opening the skin, but not perforating his intestines. A bit of blue gut peered through the wound. We captured him during the early part of a routine day-long patrol. When first taken he walked slightly doubled over holding his abdomen tightly with his hands. As he walked, more and more of his innards bubbled out. The medic initially contained them with clear protective plastic from a PRC-25 radio battery, which was tightly bound to him with a GI pistol belt. His condition worsened as he walked, doubled over holding tightly to the ever enlarging concoction with his hands and forearms. His eyes expressed pain and panic, which he bore in silence. We pitied him and I do not know his final fate after the patrol's finish.

Advancing into a gunfight near a Catholic church, ironically, I passed a very badly wounded enemy clutching the rosary around his neck and mumbling in intense prayer. The scene dismayed me; it slid into no stereotype.

ROLE MODELS

Veterans

During closing weeks of my tour SFC Juan Jose, the platoon sergeant, organized our under-strength platoon into two squads. My best friend, Fred Duncan, and I were the two squad leaders. We had a raw second lieutenant platoon leader, but he was essentially without command presence. The NCO's ran the show. Fred's DEROS preceded mine by less than a week. Sgt. Jose was leaving at that time, too. Both Fred and I, having less than two years of total service, felt quite insecure and inept in a role with life-and-death responsibility, although we were "old" soldiers – veterans with more field experience than the less senior guys in the platoon. I was a disaster with a map and compass, and was born with the directional sense of a clam. Speaking with Bruce Adams in 2003, who had been a newer member of 3rd platoon, I learned to my surprise that he and other new guys considered Fred and I seasoned veterans with practical combat experience, and they dreaded our rotation to the states.

Savvy was passed down like equipment and weapons. When Fred and I were new to Vietnam our NCO's were old career paratroopers, many being Korean War veterans like SFC Jose. A real war-horse – SSgt. Patrick O'Brien – a former instructor at Army Ranger school, had been in 3rd platoon, too. They were gone; now we walked in their boots and the fit was uncomfortable. The awesome responsibilities vested in us, the very power of life and death, is now staggering to ponder. Our civilian pursuits never rivaled such stakes. It was good that we were so young.

As a young paratrooper in 1957, O'Brien's first sergeant was Paul Huff, who received the Medal of Honor for his bravery in Italy while with the 509th Parachute Infantry in 1944. O'Brien served a total of 20 years at various times in the 50's, 60's, 70's, 80's and 90's. He completed army basic training three times, the last one at age 43. He transferred from our platoon to be a platoon sergeant in the newly minted Long Range Recon Company of the First Cavalry Division. I count coup that O'Brien asked Fred Duncan and I to transfer to be team leaders in his LRRP platoon. We were too "short" however, and would have had to extend our tours of duty to join.

O'Brien preferred using grenades at night, rather than a rifle. During one patrol we suspected imminent danger and slowly sneaked along in the dim moonlight. O'Brien led the way with a grenade in each hand, the pins pulled. A muffled cough from just ahead of us immediately attracted both of his grenades as we promptly re-routed our course.

When I finally met up with O'Brien, Jose and Collins at different times decades later, I was reminded of their normal height. In my mind they had always been ten feet tall. They remain so today. I was privileged to have had high quality leadership, especially NCOs, both in training and the 101st Airborne Division before Vietnam and during the war. They taught not only their craft but mentored simple lessons in life, – men like Korean War veteran SFC Fisher who fiercely led bayonet drill when I was a recruit. His words of wisdom: "The winner of a bayonet fight is the man who bleeds to death last." Such men are my role models for all time. Their leadership and example inspire me to this day. America needs such men. America owes them.

Perfect Ambush

    One night O'Brien led twelve of us on night ambush patrol. He set it up along a 15-foot wide trail, heightened three feet above the dry rice paddy on one side and bordered by vegetation on the other. Our ambush positions on the paddy side were concealed by a narrow screen of low bushy growth. On the opposite side of the level trail were three to four foot high meaty flat cactus plants. The kill zone was located where a 100-meter section of trail passed into an area open on our side. For us it was not unlike kneeling in front of a low theatre stage, the trail coursing the stage entrances on either side. A hooch was located on our right.

    The field of fire was ideal. Our cover and concealment was excellent. I sited my machine gun on the far left flank and drove aiming stakes, two near the muzzle and two side by side closer together set further back behind the trigger. The gun sat in between the stakes. So long as it pointed so as to sweep within the arc restricted by the stakes, the entire kill zone was blanketed with its fire even though I would be blind in the darkness. Two claymore antipersonnel mines, each with seven hundred steel balls exploding in a 60 degree arc – lethal up to fifty meters – stood sentinel at the ends, facing in towards the kill zone. I snapped in a 200 round belt of ammunition.

    A reliable and steady man, Rodney Shutts, was on the right flank and O'Brien was in the center of the ambush. His orders were clear. If enemy moved into the kill zone, no one was to fire until he detonated the claymore mines. All was ready. The night was dark and as always, spooky. Our advantage was as good as it gets and I had a feeling that we would score on this one. The conditions and set up were textbook.

Several hours later a shot busted out from the right center, instantly followed by explosions of the mines. We all opened up. I fired the entire belt, mindful to keep the machine gun muzzle depressed for low grazing fire and sweeping it right to left and back, again and again in long bursts over the entire kill zone, guided by the aiming stakes. Only hammering muzzle flashes were visible amid the noise. Shutts later told me that my fire reassured him on the right flank; the tracers passed three to four feet to his front, eighteen inches off the ground. Then the shooting sputtered out. No men could live within such fire.

But they could if they were not in it. O'Brien had not sparked the ambush. An enemy group was moving to the kill zone on Shutts' right side. He saw them and tensed for the signal. A replacement medic who was worthless, both as a medic and as a man, had heard or seen them, too. He panicked and fired his .45 pistol once. What an idiot! That single shot compromised the ambush anyway, so O'Brien triggered the claymores. Afterward I thought O'Brien would kill that medic. No one would have minded. The medic was immediately reassigned.

The ambush was, indeed, a perfect one. It lacked only enemy prey in the kill zone. Flat cactus plants on the opposite side of the trail of the kill zone resembled swiss cheese from the small arms fire and the claymore mines.

HAIRTRIGGER

Fred Duncan had true grit. I watched him risk his life to rescue two men drowning in the South China Sea. That was but one of many examples where Fred stood tall as a soldier and a man. Fred and I had become very close friends. By this time we and SFC Jose had the most time in-country in the 3rd platoon and had spent nearly the entire one-year tour together. We had been promoted to Sgt. E-5 at the same time, along with Gerald Brown, Travis Gary Walden and Anderson. Brown had rotated home; Anderson and Walden were dead. For many months Fred was RTO for our former and respected platoon leader, Lt. Chester Collins. We were always good buddies and became closer as time moved on. Fred and I discussed and described in repetitive detail all aspects of our civilian lives, childhood and high school adventures and our vision of the future. We both had college plans. It seemed as if I personally knew his brothers, parents, buddies and extended family back home in Purdin, Missouri. His affection for his family and home was contagious. Surely he felt likewise about my family. A few years later when visiting Purdin to attend his wedding, the place felt familiar to me. His family were simultaneously new acquaintances and old friends.

Three "short-timers" – Sgt. Fred Duncan, Sp 5 Bruce"Doc" Hartnell, and me on patrol 1.5 km west of Camp Radcliff.

As 3rd platoon's two squad leaders, and as best friends and real short timers, Fred and I made a pact. It was a measure of mutual regard and, I suppose, insecurity and fear, too. Time for short timers crept thick and slow, like long mid-December days to a child eager for Christmas. We yearned to go home healthy. We would watch each other's back. At that time our company was operating in a dangerous eerie area near the South China Sea. We made regular enemy contact during almost every night patrol. Fred and I agreed to volunteer to accompany any night patrol or ambush that the other was ordered to lead. Having only two squads and the platoon being required to launch an ambush patrol every night, our agreement meant long nights for Fred and me each night. It was a good trade and cemented our friendship forever.

Worst Moment

One dimly moonlit night I went along with Fred Duncan and his squad on a 10-man ambush patrol. Fred was in the lead and I was next to the last in the file. As we neared the ambush location, a trail junction in a flat open area near a graveyard interposed with manioc plots, Fred and Schmidt left the rest of us in place while they moved in closer to the site to scout the best ambush position. They wore bush hats; Fred was short and Schmidt was taller. I remained with the patrol which stayed put in a manioc plot, alert and silently standing in single file. I was facing forward.

Shortly the worst moment of my life occurred. The man behind me fired one round, grunted and hit the ground to give me a field of fire. His M-16 had jammed. In an instant as I spun around I saw the lineaments of two men in the lambent moonlight just a few yards away moving perpendicular to the course of our patrol. Reacting immediately, I fired my M-16 rifle on full automatic at them as I spun to face rearward. So many months in the field had shifted my reflexes to automatic, too. In my split second flashbulb image each spectre wore bush hats and one was taller than the other. There was no return fire. Almost instantly, as I quit firing I knew that I had just shot Fred and Schmidt. Of course, I thought, returning from their recon they slightly overshot our location and came up behind us. I was completely stunned – paralyzed with remorse, dread and self-loathing. My mind visited the funeral home and I conjured a sepia-toned image of Fred's parents and family in deep mourning, and my duty to be there and tell them how Fred had died. Never could I muster the courage to do that. Immediate suicide was the only viable option, the path of honor and least resistance. My mind moved to it naturally, logically and at once. These thoughts occurred either in a flash, or over a period of seconds or several minutes. I do not know. Time was as warped and distorted as my composure and equilibrium. Not only was my best friend dead after enduring almost a whole year in that place, cheated from that great homecoming we all imagined, he died at my hand.

I still hear the wonderful words. Fred pulled on my shoulder whispering, "Steve, what happened?" He and Schmidt had hurried back after the shooting. No sunrise has ever been brighter, no pain killer ever gave more relief than those words. Fred was alive and well. It was a North Vietnamese patrol I had fired at after all. Such elation!

But were there more NVA? Muzzle flashes from more firing on our part would pinpoint us. Fred and I loathed to venture out and check for enemy bodies, so we collected all the hand grenades from the patrol. Then he and I crawled nearer to where the NVA had been or were, hunkered behind the butt ends of long two-foot-high sand windrows in the manioc field, and we heaved the grenades towards the NVA. We still laugh that some of them exploded between each other's windrow cover, the open space between them were troughs for secondary shrapnel jetting by our bodies. I was giddy that he was alive. I have no memory of other events that night, but in the early morning light we spotted a blood trail and drag marks where the enemy had escaped with their casualties.

Friendship

Emotionally my mind programmed that I killed my best friend. Even though the mistake endured momentarily, it was my worst life experience. My guts still roil when I think hard on it. Each time I see Fred and his family I go back to Vietnam and imagine what could have happened and what for me did happen, if only for a little while. A part of that dreadful moment is still here.

Our mutual adventures did not end in Vietnam. Fred's stateside assignment was to the 82nd Airborne Division at Ft. Bragg, North Carolina. The army sent me to the 101st Airborne Division at Ft. Campbell, Kentucky. Then in September of 1967 it transferred me to the 82nd. By a surprising coincidence I was posted to C Company, 2nd Battalion, 504th Infantry, not only the same rifle company, but the same platoon as Fred.

Slated for a night jump, our names appeared on the manifest for a C-141 Starlifter cargo jet along with only one young cherry jumper. That aircraft was probably capable of carrying 75 paratroopers, but only three of us loaded in. None of us was jumpmaster qualified – something was wrong here – but we went ahead. On each military parachute jump, a jumpmaster-qualified soldier has command and responsibility. This jump was unique. I never knew the reason for the absence of a jumpmaster or why only three jumpers were aboard. But it was fun. After three hours of flight the air force crew chief gave us a five minute warning. We hooked up to the static line, checked equipment and let that cherry stand in the door – a real thrill for his first non-qualifying jump. The pilot cut the two inboard jet engines, deployed the wind deflector beside the forward portion of the door and we jumped into the starry night.

Fred honored me as the best man at his wedding a few years later. My daughter, Abigail, and his son, Tyler, have been friends since childhood.

30

INSTINCTS

Jacob's Ladder

Our physical reactions were hairtrigger; Vietnam honed other senses and in some men they became razor sharp. My friend Shutts, for instance, had a nose for water. In order to clear an LZ in canopied jungle, 3rd platoon was inserted via a "Jacobs Ladder." It dangled from a Chinook CH-47 double bladed helicopter hovering 50 feet above the jungle floor through a hole in the jungle canopy created by a B-52 blast. The ladder had cable side rails. We climbed out the rear ramp down the rolled-out ladder. My load included an M-79 20 mm grenade launcher with 20 grenades, an M-16 with 200 rounds for it, and 200 rounds of machine gun ammo. The weight of several men and their loads on the ladder caused it to angle inward. The descent was an effort. An RTO fell, landing on his back, but escaped injury. Cutting an LZ in the dense vegetation was hard parching work. All searched the jungle for a water source to no avail. Shutts then led two of us to a cool spring-fed pool no larger than a dinner plate 50 yards into the bush. Such refreshment! It was partially covered with leaves. How did he find it? With a tooth-sucking demure understatement he claimed that he smelled it. It was impossible for him to have seen it. Shutts always heard furtive noises before any one else, too. He had intuition. He went home alive and in one piece.

Signs

You learn to read signs. Deserted warm cook fires have meaning. You study your prey. In one area C Company was established on an artillery fire base from which it conducted daily patrols and set ambushes. For several days helicopters arrived with hot chow at the same time each day and then our patrols were called in to eat. That was the time, we discovered, when the enemy moved. One day 3rd platoon stayed on patrol when chow came in. We wounded two and captured one baby-faced NVA armed with AK-47s. The enemy has a distinct odor. Your nose often warned they were or had been near. They likely recognized our odor, too. Your body stays tense even if you feel you are not. The eyes, ears, and gut are antenna tuned to clues and signals of danger like never before. Over thirty years later I began to regularly hike in the woods. Dormant habits quickened. Primitive sensors – a sharpened sense of sight and an eye for furtive movement – returned. I automatically search the trees and trail ahead, eyes sweeping for sign – without thinking.

When we broke our patrol routine these NVA were caught moving in the open.

What happened to the unwary? What befell those heedless of signs? Here is an example. Up the valley west of our platoon perimeter, Ft. Lonely, a small ancient pagoda nestled among bamboo and abandoned paddy terraces. Stained and patinaed with time, unkempt with disuse, it had that forever-look of a castle. An aura of timelessness seeped from eye-catching gargoyles and dragon-motif spires. Nature had lost the attempt to reclaim it. The interior shrine was intact. Thick straw matted the floor. Several relics lay scattered about. None were disturbed or looted. Don't tempt an omen – a holy place can cast a curse.

The temple fronted the valley facing the South China Sea a few miles away. Several switchback footpaths snaked down from the mountains and coiled together nearby onto a wide trail 200 meters distant. Six of us were sent here on a hunch. Third platoon had been positioned a half mile away for many days. Maybe the pagoda would be a good venue for an observation post. From there the source of a main trail was in direct line of sight. But we really did not expect to see any bad guys.

The pagoda was almost cozy. We slept wrapped up in our ponchos on the dry straw as the rain pattered outside. Two of us at a time alternated around-the-clock watch from comfortable concealment on the terra-cotta tile roof. A low stuccoed masonry balustrade surrounded the sweeping decorative roof edge. Beautifully ugly gargoyles, pitted and blemished with age, silently sneered and ranted from their ancestral perches atop the roof wall. It was exotic – a scene from *Tarzan* or *Indiana Jones*.

I looked forward to a few relaxing restful days sheltered here, trail watching from our commanding elevation like a cat on a porch rail. Surely news of GI activity in the valley flashed through the enemy's grapevine. Surely none would foolishly attempt a daylight movement near us – and not on a main trail. Surely they realized GI patrols, ambushes and observations posts tentacled the area. Surely the furtive helicopter flights in and out of C Company headquarters near the beach broadcast danger.

The maxim "10% never get the word" – true in the U.S. Army – was also true in the enemy forces. Idling on the roof on the second day, my buddy and I perked up when a lone enemy soldier armed with a M-1 carbine strode onto the trail. I grabbed the radio handset and made reservations for him with the 3rd platoon. If he remained on course he would arrive in fifteen minutes. He walked on. A squad from 3rd platoon dry-gulched him. Read sign or die. A few hours later we spied two more VC moving in the same direction. Same drill. It cost one his life. Be wary or die. Our pagoda bunch saddled up and moved out. En route to Ft. Lonely we casually passed the two sprawled in death – blind to sign and now forever oblivious.

31

PARTING SHOT

    For his last cut at me, the Grim Reaper's scythe sliced just shy of my guts. It was a solid lunge delivered during my last minutes in a combat zone. This was my big day and everyone knew it. A man's rotation date was public lore, amplified and bragged over by the proud owner more frequently as the magic day approached. He would tease, boasting such things as "Two days, a wake-up, and the duffel bag drag – and I'm on that freedom bird to the world," or "I'm so short I could sit on the edge of toilet paper and dangle my feet." Being so short conferred a celebrity status, you were the envy of all. Newer guys, called "cherries," looked upon you with awe. To them you represented hope that they too, may survive intact and return home. I thought it bad luck to flaunt such good fortune and did not tease fate. One should never cackle until the egg is laid firmly into the nest. During my last week in the field, I dug a one-man shallow foxhole each night large enough to sleep in.

    Our detachment had a morning patrol on my final day. As I readied for this last one, dirty minds pondered the cruel ironies scripted for short timers on that mortal stage – would it be my very last walk? Just ask that sergeant, who after fifteen hard months, lost an eye to grenade fragments on his last day. And Walden was killed after surviving for 11 months. Then SSgt. Lacy Watts told me to stand down. I would go out on the next chopper in with hot chow and mail. Two days later I would sit in my parents' living room, safe and dry. Imagine if you were to walk on Mars two days from today. The transition is equally stark and dramatic. Homecoming was an almost impossible dream yearned for for 365 days and nights, a vision ricocheting from daydream to night dream and back.

The patrol moved out. I lazed near the LZ, my back resting on a paddy dike, ankles crossed, my ears cocked for whispers of slapping chopper blades in the distance. The sky stayed silent. In a few hours the patrol returned. Bruce "Doc" Hartnell, a Wisconsinite and my oldest friend remaining with the platoon after a year of cruel and constant human gains and discards, approached with a grin. He had recovered enough from his wounds to hightail it back to 3rd platoon after they choppered Dougher's body to the evac hospital.

Doc was encumbered with a bulky green medic's kit, his bag of miracles, and thus was armed with only a .45 pistol. Besides, his real job did not involve outgoing rounds. Noting my disappointment at the tardy helicopter transport, as he unfastened his pistol belt, he said: "Steve, sad to see you still here," and tossed it down in front of me. When it struck the ground the pistol fired through the holster into the dike wall next to me – the bullet striking just over a foot beside my belly. Doc, flushed red and speechless, turned and walked away. Silence hung in the air. He had fired the weapon during the patrol. A round had remained chambered. The safety had not been engaged. The choppers came soon. I was gone. C Company was mortared that night. There were several wounded.

32

HOME ALIVE

Jousting with Doc Hartnell's .45 made my final moments in the boonies unforgettable. Tradition held that a short timer's last chopper ride to the rear area be memorable. The pilot was traditional. He made banking turns, then dove to a river lined with palm trees. The slick dropped below tree-top height and rocked to and fro as it slid like a blur between the trees following the meanders of the river. It was thrilling. I savored that I was homeward bound and not bleeding or in a bag. But there was a bothersome hair of anxiety on my tongue.

Two days later the wild cheers of a planeload of stateside-bound GIs delighted my ears as the wheels lifted from Vietnam. We were allowed to deplane at the Honolulu refueling stop. Our status as human cattle did not change on home soil. At the terminal a bathroom was cordoned off for our use and we were forbidden to mingle with or speak to civilians. Were we not returning as proud Americans, thinking we had done something good? Civilians seemed to view us as wild creatures. A self-consciousness and sense of lower stature was settling in, a coarse penance for a hard year.

Every rear echelon bar phony whines that he was spit on when he deplaned in the states. No one spit on us. Had someone done so, he would not have expectorated again between original teeth. An enduring "moon" to the fake heroes!

Oakland Army base near San Francisco offered a hot shower, a new Class A uniform and a steak, the first and last steak that I ever declined. It was after midnight and I was anxious to get a flight to Chicago. At the airport I met buddies I had not seen since

Ft. Campbell and some with whom I had trained. They had served in several different airborne units in Vietnam and we swapped information on the fate of others. SSgt. Little, a Guamanian, an NCO from my old company in the 101st Airborne at Ft. Campbell whom I respected, greeted me as a peer. I had heard he had been killed and was happy to prove the rumor false.

I sweat in anticipation as the plane landed at O'Hare where my bride-to-be was waiting with her classy new 1967 Ford Mustang. She was as patient and understanding as she remains after almost 40 years of toil and triumph together. I was unaccustomed to ashtrays and with a three-pack-a-day habit, I needed to learn not to flick ashes on the carpet of her new car. All of the rules changed overnight. Civilian habits needed to be relearned, recent ones forgotten – the most obvious being my choice of adjectives. No more squatting to crap on the ground – sidearm handy. No need to spring alive with any loud noise. My leave passed quickly and Denise and I married on June 24, 1967 and honeymooned for two days en route to Ft. Campbell, Kentucky. One year remained on my three-year enlistment.

Within three days of nearly being gut shot in Vietnam, I sat uneasily in my parent's living room. In coming days Bob Green, a close family friend, asked me a question about helicopter air assaults and Joe Boyle thanked me and shook my hand through the driver's window on his service pickup. Naturally, people ignored the 500 pound gorilla in the room; me too. I harbored a dark knowledge of certain ways of the real world and needed to convince myself otherwise. As kids we learn to ride bikes and to pretend, and we never forget how.

Adjustment

Silent internal sensors remained unconvinced. I had not decompressed. My senses and nervous system were still doing time in 3rd platoon, though at the time the phenomenon remained unacknowledged. The first night at home was sleepless. A soft bed was useless. There was a hassle about sleeping in a corner on the floor, so by morning I slept on Grandpa's picnic table beneath the mulberry tree. The rituals and rhythm of infantry existence in Vietnam were ground in deeper than the dirt in my skin. Walking at night in my hometown without a weapon, I was incomplete and vulnerable. My eyes swept the sidewalk for trip wires. I cupped my nighttime cigarettes for months. Hyper-vigilance persisted in some ways for years. Jungle rot and ringworm still annoyed my skin and I had gut issues. My body grime ringed the tub even after several baths. None of this was reassuring or esteeming. I was a turd at the cotillion.

Ten days later a soft bunk was tolerable. As I dozed on the couch one afternoon, mother shook me for supper. In a wink I had her down on the floor by the neck. How do you apologize for or

Newlyweds at our apartment in Clarksville, TN July 1967.

explain that? At age 20 you ignore that it happened. Later my young bride would be bewildered by similar behavior. I was a freak. Then one night at Ft. Campbell in the 502nd Infantry where about half of the men had recently returned from Vietnam, I had CQ (charge of quarters) duty inspecting the platoon bays and arms rooms every hour. The barracks sounded like a zoo. Screams, cries and every other dream sound came forth from dozens of sleeping GIs. There was no choice then but to see the humor in it, and hoodwink yourself.

Timewarp

During my leave several high school classmates were kind to invite me to Madison for a college-scene beerfest. It was enjoyable, but like the whore in church, I was out of place. The past year lasted only 12 months for them, but was a decade for me. I felt like I had been everywhere and done everything. Subtle invisible forces encouraged forgetting what I had seen and denying their emotional effects. These scenes were disorienting if I was not careful. Everything at home was the same – everything at home was different. It is easy to confuse reality so I isolated myself. It was not possible to relate to those who had not had a similar experience. I seldom interacted with non-family members, except for pre-war friends. During four years of college I studied and roamed campus anonymously, interacting with few people not directly related to academic matters. I missed my Vietnam friends. The war had not stopped in Vietnam either. Shouldn't I have stayed?

33

REFLECTIONS

Gain

Withstanding hazardous combat and its privation and squalor confers self confidence and a novel sense of self-worth. You have passed an ultimate rite of passage in military culture. You humped your load and carried your weight. You had not let your buddies down. You stood it and have a mute pride of personal achievement. Meeting a challenge to your survival gratifies; being shot at and missed is exhilarating. The CIB, Combat Infantryman's Badge, awarded for being in infantry combat, is a respected award and one of the few with real meaning. I wear a miniature lapel CIB. These credits do not transfer to any civilian pursuit or social milieu.

You grow up immediately in some ways. War removes the "me" in you and sometimes even the "why me?" Your background, social status, education or future prospects become irrelevant. You are a blank page when you arrive there. Former nobodies become important and would-be tough guys fold. Excuses do not matter, results do. Only performance counts. Mistakes, whatever the cause, may mean that people die or are hurt. Fate and luck are beyond control, but behavior can make luck. You live close to the bone, shorn of the extraneous and non-essential. You shed all niceties of civilized life. You find your core. If you adapt properly and have luck – you keep it.

In Vietnam the grim circumstances and the uncertainty of my immediate future lent a certain vividness to the present. Mundane or ordinary pleasures heighten. Food does not taste better, but you enjoy it more. Sleep is sounder, jokes are funnier. Life is rich when you live for the moment.

An infantryman at war has an opportunity to observe all facets of human nature, from the best to the worst. Although boots, weapons and gear are standard army issue you can recognize a man by such items like you know a classmate's handwriting. Each boot has that certain scuff or wear mark, and gear is arranged or frayed uniquely. A scratch or cracked stock signifies a weapon's bearer. Likewise character is revealed. War calibrated my judgment of character. To this day I unwittingly measure people by an estimation of how they might have handled themselves in our outfit. You really know men there, even if you dislike them.

Prolonged stress reduces men to their genuine elements and exposes them. There was an absence of empty and meaningless manners or airs; speech was profane, but direct. A man under pressure reveals character traits, good and bad, that otherwise would not bob up to the surface. You see acts of brutality of the worst sort. You see feats of courage of the best sort. You feel strokes of fear and doubt. You find pluck and mettle. You go beyond yourself. War made me loath pretension and mere appearance. Trendiness and fashion lose meaning. What would my close army buddies accept? That's how I judge myself. We did not crave the finer things. We were not wine snobs and never would be. You realize how transparent and empty many aspects of so-called civilization and society truly are. It made me unenvious of wealth and appreciative of value.

Cost

The experience of infantry war exacts a heavy price, though, even for survivors. Memory of war is like a pocket full of shattered glass. You recoil in pain if you shove a hand in, but the pieces eventually poke where it hurts if not deftly removed. War is killing and mayhem; no politically correct euphemisms soften the cold reality – an infantryman remembers how it is. A narrow-horizoned public oriented to the short term would not stand for war, if it knew the reality. You lose some of your humanity. You learn the facts of life and death and appreciate the precariousness of life as most other young people do not. War makes a divide with those that have not done it. The experience is ineffable, you cannot find the words to relate it to others so you do not try. After Vietnam they did not seem to care. Veterans returned to a recriminatory public, anyway. I stuffed it down, encapsulating a desolate heartbreak. It made me feel like an outcast and I struggled to fit into any group, or social situation, or circumstance, but remained adrift. Teeny-bopper college bullshit held no shine for me. You are more withdrawn and unable or reluctant to disclose or release your mind. You choose few new friends. None can be as solid and as trustworthy as those you had there.

34

LESSONS

I moved through the Vietnam War as an observer rather than a participant. Only my eyes and ears were involved. The war unfolded in otherworldliness and the real me seemed to float above and outside the action. But my sentiments and passions were entangled down there. For long years I labored to shift these perceptions to the front of my brain to digest, analyze, and process these early profound events for useful accommodation into normal life. Like Scarlett O'Hara, I would *really* think about Vietnam tomorrow. It is a dead-lift chore. Wringing memory, wheedling recollection – wallowed in emotion – I sort through freshened images, and grab at vision phantoms to tease out the meaning. I need the footing for a totem of personal insight and understanding. Only the hole is dug. I am disappointed that the experience is not now resolved cleanly, as I had so long hoped and assumed it would be.

I am annoyed with myself for harboring hard and difficult feelings from the war. They are unwarranted. I was not drafted or threatened with imminent draft. Had I enrolled in college in 1965, a student draft deferment would have exempted me for at least four years. Then I would have been subject to the first draft lottery. My number was 366 – the best possible. No career or employment opportunity was interrupted. I was single. The timing of my enlistment was my choice, as was my branch – airborne infantry. I served at a most opportune time, immediately after high school graduation. I returned from the war physically unscathed. There is no cause for complaint or regret and I voice none. I asked for it. Yet there is a silent undefined anger tinged with bitterness that I cannot trace, other than that the public devalued such service. One must accept war as past, although it seems ever-present, and embrace the strength and perspective it offers to battle future challenges. You may elegize the sacrifice and friendships while condemning the circumstance.

As I reflect, there comes a nostalgia for the simplicity and odd freedom of having and needing only those things carried on your back and knowing exactly who your real friends were and how each would perform. At that point of the war we young paratroopers had no doubts. Neither the luxury nor the inclination to debate the pros and cons of the war were available. We were still bloated with a hubris that would puncture for our replacements in the years to come, along with America's resolve.

The ground war was young in 1966-67 and those with whom I trained and fought were true believers. It has been said that America originally fielded a top-quality army in Vietnam. But the war's length, the type of personnel rotation and nature of infantry combat weakened its professional NCO core. Those I fought with did not become the mangy malcontents depicted in cinema and the media. It is a mark of personal pride that we were the equal, though 20 years younger, of the like of those who jumped into Normandy, held Bastogne and secured Saipan. My buddies had the right stuff and offered themselves up, bore many a burden, paid a high price because they thought it was the right thing to do and because they were Airborne.

I had become a man while I was still a teenager there and had developed a hard edge with a sense that there was little I could not do. Life's most powerful experience was over and my whole life was yet to be lived. Summer road and masonry construction work as a laborer was a cinch. Seven years of college and law school were uncomplicated and required only application of self-discipline.

More than most young people, I knew how wonderful it was just to be alive. I had literally burned shit and figuratively eaten shit. The face of death had appeared in several forms. Vietnam revealed the intense and lasting camaraderie of young men which is born of shared adversity and danger. I bumped up against American values – loyalty, courage, honor, individual responsibility and self-sacrifice – that were going stale back home. It was a graduate study in the human condition. As an infantryman, I sat in the front row at the academy of self-mastery and self-knowledge. The tuition was high, but no amount of material wealth compares to the value of that education. The credits are priceless. I learned to sift genuine worth from the chaff of consumer culture and earned a master's degree in humility. At middle age it is a challenge to keep such lessons connected to a modern life of ease and plenty. But they have daily application.

35

AMERICA - STILL THE BEAUTIFUL

The merits of the Vietnam War, the hottest battle of the long Cold War, are beyond this narrative, however . . . ***Let those who hated us for doing our duty review the events following the final humiliating U.S. withdrawal from Vietnam in 1975:***

- Millions died in the killing fields of Cambodia.
- Two million South Vietnamese fled their homeland. Thousands died in the exodus.
- Tens of thousands came to the United States.
- A million of the abandoned and stay-behinds were imprisoned in "re-education" camps for over a decade. Many were the best and brightest young leaders. Thousands died there.
- Vietnam became a closed impoverished client state. It was a stooge of the Soviets.
- To a myopic America the absence of war tricked an illusion of peace.

History will gaze more favorably upon us who *fought* the war than leaders who orchestrated it or those who opposed it. On balance the experience for me was a source of strength. I gained knowledge of people and the world that an urbane lifetime of civility could not provide. The war at home and within was my real challenge, especially while the hot war raged on, and many of our countrymen disdained Vietnam veterans and our service. An aching bitterness of betrayal trespassed into me. My loving wife and university studies guided me through.

This account relates only fragments of memory and impressions from that pivotal era. Much of it remains unsaid. Some you would not believe. Much of it I do not understand. What is certain is my duty to record and reflect upon what I do understand – what some baby-boomer men and boys gave there. The motivation has been to relate the defining point of my life to my girls. In the process I hacked up some nasty emotional hairballs. A few litter this account. My stern experiences induced me during their childhood, to over-emphasize life's potential to be bleak and dangerous, and to over-stress the importance of earnest self-sufficiency and self-discipline. Each of them brought a brilliance of light into my life. I impressed on them my view that the world is harsh. They taught me that it is wonderful.

POSTSCRIPT

I visited the Vietnam Veteran's Memorial in 1990 and was impressed that my late friends' names had somehow carried from the obscurity of their sacrifice in that forsaken land across the globe to the national capitol. My eyes studied those letters carved into the polished black granite, and then appeared a profound and moving juxtaposition: my own reflection staring back through them. The tribute is fitting.